The Foreign Policy Puzzle

The Foreign Policy Puzzle

Interests, Threats, and Tools

KEITH SHIMKO
PURDUE UNIVERSITY

New York   Oxford
OXFORD UNIVERSITY PRESS

Oxford University Press is a department of the University of Oxford.
It furthers the University's objective of excellence in research,
scholarship, and education by publishing worldwide.

Oxford   New York
Auckland   Cape Town   Dar es Salaam   Hong Kong   Karachi
Kuala Lumpur   Madrid   Melbourne   Mexico City   Nairobi
New Delhi   Shanghai   Taipei   Toronto

With offices in
Argentina   Austria   Brazil   Chile   Czech Republic   France   Greece
Guatemala   Hungary   Italy   Japan   Poland   Portugal   Singapore
South Korea   Switzerland   Thailand   Turkey   Ukraine   Vietnam

For titles covered by Section 112 of the US Higher Education
Opportunity Act, please visit www.oup.com/us/he for the
latest information about pricing and alternate formats.

Published by Oxford University Press
198 Madison Avenue, New York, New York 10016
http://www.oup.com

Oxford is a registered trademark of Oxford University Press.

The CIP Data is On-File at the Library of Congress.

ISBN: 978-0-19-998877-8

Printing number: 9 8 7 6 5 4 3 2 1

Printed in Canada on acid-free paper

*To Stanley Michalak and in memory of
Glenn Miller, both of Franklin and Marshall College.
Even after all these years, this book reflects
what I learned from them.*

BRIEF TABLE OF CONTENTS

TABLE OF CONTENTS

....

ACKNOWLEDGMENTS

The author is grateful to the editorial, design, and marketing staff at Oxford University Press. We particularly appreciate the efforts of Jennifer Carpenter, Tony Mathias, Simon Benjamin, Michele Laseau, and Matt Rohal, among others including, Michael Kopf, the production manager of the project.

We owe a debt of gratitude, as well, to the following people, who reviewed the manuscript in its development and who gave generously of their time and expertise:

Mark A. Cichok, *University of Texas at Arlington*
Eric Fattor, *Colorado State University*
Patrick J. Haney, *Miami University*
Michael Huelshoff, *University of New Orleans*
Michael D. Kanner, *University of Colorado, Boulder*
James M. Lutz, *Indiana University–Purdue University at Fort Wayne*
Ekaterina Levintova, *University of Wisconsin–Green Bay*
Zachary Selden, *University of Florida*
James Seroka, *Auburn University*
John W. Sutherlin, *University of Louisiana at Monroe*
Edwin Taylor, *Missouri Western State University*

The book would not have been the same without the assistance and insight from these outstanding scholars and teachers. Meanwhile, any errors you may find in the book remain our own. We welcome your feedback and thank you for your support.

PREFACE

....

A lthough this book has been only two years in the writing, it has been more than thirty years in the making. I have thought about it as long as I have been a professor, teacher, and actively engaged citizen. As a result, my debts are many and varied. They begin with Stanley Michalak and the late Glenn Miller of Franklin and Marshall College, to whom this book is dedicated. Even after all these years, no one has been more important in terms of the way I think about foreign policy and international politics. Most important, they inspired me to pursue a career of research and teaching that has brought me to this point. More immediately, Bert Rockman got the ball rolling on this project when he approached me about writing an accessible book exploring the central problems of U.S. foreign policy, something I had always wanted to do. I am grateful to Jennifer Carpenter of Oxford University Press for her initial and continuing interest in the project as well as her patience as I struggled with it. I would like to thank William Shelby, my research assistant. That big binder of material he produced turned a task that might have taken two or three months into one that only took a few weeks. He should be viewed as my coauthor on the case studies appearing at the end of Chapters 2, 3, and 4. Finally, the anonymous reviewers of the original prospectus and final manuscript provided constructive criticism that made the book before you better in many respects.

INTRODUCTION
....

A successful book needs at least three things. First, and perhaps most obvious, it should have a well-defined subject that can be addressed adequately within its confines. A sprawling thousand-page magnum opus can be wide ranging and exhaustive, whereas a book a fraction of that length requires a more narrow and selective focus. Second, it needs an objective, a reason for being, a clear idea of what the reader is supposed to get from it. Finally, it should be written with an audience in mind, some idea of who is likely to read it and why. This is important because even books on the same general subject can vary greatly in content and orientation depending on the intended audience. People want and need to know different things based on their relationship with the subject. There can, for example, be several versions of an automobile manual for the same model car depending on whether it is written for factory workers who assemble it, mechanics who might need to repair it, or owners who operate it. No doubt the various manuals will cover a lot of common ground, but they will also be tailored to meet specific needs. As the car's owner, I might refer to my manual to learn what the flashing warning lights on the dashboard mean, but I do not need to know how to fix every malfunction they indicate. I need to know when the brake pads are worn so I can take the car into the shop, not how to replace them myself. So at the outset it useful to answer three questions: What is this book about? What is its objective? Who is the audience?

What's the Subject?

This is a book about foreign policy, American foreign policy in particular. But this does not really tell us much because the subject is so broad and varied. There are, for example, hundreds, probably thousands, of foreign policy books that are essentially diplomatic histories, from sweeping overviews stretching back to the origins of the republic to extremely detailed narratives of particular decisions, policies, periods, crises, issues, or relationships. Other foreign policy books examine the process by which foreign policy is made and the actors/forces that shape it, explaining the powers of the president versus Congress, the impact of public opinion, the influence of interest groups, the role of bureaucracies, and so on, with an eye toward understanding why American foreign policy is what it is. There are surveys of contemporary problems confronting policy makers such as terrorism, the rise of China, the global recession, and protecting/promoting human rights, often presented in a debate format. Finally, there are works of policy advocacy making a case for the author's strategy or vision. This book is none of these things.

Understanding what this book is about begins with recognizing what might appear too obvious to mention: foreign policy is public policy, and like any other policy—economic policy, health-care policy, or environmental policy—it presents both intellectual and political challenges. The challenges are intellectual in that people need to think about what policy should be. They must specify objectives and priorities, understand the nature of the problem the policy is supposed to address, identify policy options and anticipate their consequences, and, finally, choose the policy most likely to achieve the desired objectives. The result is rarely unanimity or even consensus. Even if people go through the same basic intellectual process, debates about policy emerge because they invariably answer one or more of the critical questions differently along the way. The experience with the Affordable Care Act, more commonly referred to as "Obamacare," provides a typical example: there were disagreements at virtually every point from the objectives of health-care reform (e.g., maximizing freedom of choice or achieving universal coverage) to the anticipated consequences of proposed legislation (e.g., would it exacerbate or restrain the upward trajectory of health-care costs and premiums?). Such is the nature of policy debates.

There is, of course, more to policy making than thinking through the issues. As even the most casual observer of American politics knows, the process by which public policy is decided and implemented rarely resembles a model of dispassionate intellectual analysis. The policies governments eventually enact are the result of an often messy political processes through which competing preferences are translated into public policy. Again, one need look no further than the process by which the Affordable Care Act was legislated and implemented to see just how messy all of this can be. This is where the political challenges of policy come into play. Just because a policy makes the most intellectual sense does not guarantee that it will prevail in the political contest.

In the larger scheme of policy analysis, the intellectual challenges are most relevant when we are interested in what policy *ought to* be, whereas the political challenges and processes relate primarily to understanding what policy *actually is*. Although the political and intellectual elements of policy making are equally important, this book focuses on the intellectual side of the equation. This is a book about American foreign policy in that it provides the conceptual foundations for thinking systematically about what the nation's foreign policy ought to be. It develops a rough map for navigating the complex intellectual terrain of foreign policy, emphasizing the major roads and critical forks where difficult decisions must be made while highlighting and illustrating that hazards frequently encountered along various routes. But it must be stressed that it is only a map, not a set of directions. Maps do not tell people where they are headed or where they should go. Maps help people get their bearings in unfamiliar surroundings.

What's the Objective?

This map metaphor goes a long way in conveying what the book seeks to accomplish—that is, what readers are supposed to get out of it. The objective is relatively, perhaps deceptively, simple, even if the subject matter is anything but—to provide the intellectual tools for thinking systematically and carefully about the central problems of foreign policy. It presents a framework focusing on the critical issues to be addressed in thinking about the United States' role in the world. It is a framework that serves a dual purpose. First, it can help guide and clarify one's own thinking about American foreign policy by bringing order and focus to complex issues and problems. Second, it can serve as a template for analyzing and evaluating the positions and arguments of others, a device to help understand why and how policy makers and analysts arrive at sometimes wildly divergent responses to the same foreign policy problems.

The framework is most usefully viewed as a series of questions. Reflecting its dual purposes, these questions can be used for self-reflection, asked of ourselves as we think about foreign policy, or for interrogation, posed to others whose views we want to understand and analyze. Of course, in many cases it is not possible to ask the questions directly since most people do not have personal interactions with the president or secretary of state. We are normally exposed to policy debates indirectly through editorials, opinion essays, commentary, speeches, and interviews with policy makers. We must look for answers that may or may not be provided. Since no one is required to answer our questionnaire, this often requires a little detective work and reading between the lines.

The framework and questions it encourages us to ask and answer reflect three of the most fundamental and enduring intellectual challenges in foreign policy—conceptualizing, identifying, and prioritizing American *interests*; assessing the nature and magnitude of *threats* to these interests; and evaluating the relative effectiveness of the various *tools of influence* available to policy makers in defending/promoting these interests. Whether operating at the level of grand strategy (i.e., an overall vision of the United States' role in the world) or that of responses to specific problems, there is no escaping questions about interests, threats, and tools. And debates about foreign policy, whether it is the wisdom of attacking Iraq in 2003, intervening in the Syrian conflict, or countering Putin's moves in Crimea and Ukraine, are almost always rooted in disagreements about the interests at stake, the nature of the threat, and/or the most effective tools to employ. So asking oneself and others about American interests, threats to those interests, and the appropriate policy tools allows us to clarify our own views, analyze the arguments of others, and make sense of policy debates.

Who's the Audience?

There is another sense in which foreign policy resembles other areas of public policy: debates about policy are often overwhelming and difficult to disentangle. Average citizens, most of whom have neither the time nor the inclination to spend hours upon hours mastering all the details of policy, are usually confronted with a bewildering range of confident, informed, and sincere "experts" of all political persuasions bombarding them with a seemingly endless barrage of competing and contradictory arguments. This is confusing enough in domestic policy but probably worse with regard to foreign policy because most people have less firsthand experience with the issues. At least issues in the domestic arena are often more tangible: people see the taxes withheld from paychecks, receive unemployment insurance, observe the consequences of failing to comply with laws, and deal with health-care providers and insurance companies. In many cases people can figure out how alternative domestic policies would affect them, which provides some foundation for evaluation.

This is occasionally the case in foreign policy as well. With trade agreements, for example, people working in industries threatened or helped by opening markets can easily imagine the consequences. But on many foreign policy issues this is more difficult. How many people know much about the details of the conflict in Syria or who the major players and factions are? Probably very few. Do many have a real sense of how the outcome in Syria might alter the politics of a region where the United States has allies and interests? Probably not. As a result, it is usually easier for most people to make sense of domestic policy debates because they have more direct experience with the policies in question and are likely to have somewhat greater knowledge. Because the issues are usually less familiar and more remote, making sense of foreign policy can be challenging. It is more difficult for people to envision how they might be affected by the outcome of a conflict elsewhere in the world than they would be by having their taxes raised or being required to purchase health insurance. Compared to domestic policy, foreign policy problems are by their very nature, well, foreign to most people.

This is a book for those who find themselves in this situation. It is written for the interested and informed, if somewhat perplexed, citizen who wants to understand why policy makers, analysts, and pundits find it so difficult to agree about the United States' role in the world generally or how it should respond to specific events or crises. It can be viewed as a sort of primer—an introduction to the fundamentals, the most important issues, questions, and dilemmas that confront anyone thinking about the American foreign policy. Returning to the roadmap metaphor, the focus is on the major highways, streets, and intersections, not every back alley or off-ramp. The objective is to identify enduring questions and dilemmas while explaining and illustrating why they are so important and difficult to answer or resolve—that is, why they are, and will certainly remain, *enduring* questions and dilemmas driving foreign policy debates. The goal is not to answer the questions or resolve the dilemmas. This is book about *how* to think about foreign policy, not *what* to think.

Invitations to Struggle

Edwin Corwin once famously observed that the institutional structure of American government, based on shared/separated powers and checks and balances, is an "invitation to struggle for the privilege of directing American foreign policy."[1] Virtually every use of military force, for example, is accompanied by the familiar debate about where the president's powers as commander in chief end and the Congress's authority and responsibility to declare war begin. The president may negotiate treaties but the Senate must ratify them. And any foreign policy that costs money requires a congressional appropriation of funds. Corwin was no doubt correct that part of the conflict surrounding foreign policy derives from the American system of governance. The same can be said of economic, social, health care, or any other policy, although the nature of the struggle can vary from one policy arena to another depending on how the pertinent powers are distributed. Health-care and economic policy are different than foreign policy in that there is nothing quite comparable to the president's powers as commander in chief in these areas. Nonetheless, Corwin's insight is by no means limited to foreign policy. The separation of powers is an invitation to struggle over any/every policy.

If this were a book about the process of foreign policy making, it would deal with these institutional conflicts and dynamics in great detail. But it is not. The focus here is on a different but no less important struggle. In reality, foreign policy involves at least two invitations and struggles. Corwin's was an invitation to the *political* struggle surrounding American foreign policy, a contest involving the power and prerogatives of the actors and institutions that shape, influence, and

---

1. Cecil V. Crabb and Pat M. Holt, *Invitation to Struggle: Congress, the President and American Foreign Policy* (Washington, D.C.: CQ Press, 1989).

determine policy. The intensity and importance of these conflicts, however, varies with the degree of agreement/disagreement about the
policy itself. If the president and Congress agree about the content of
policy, there need not be much of a struggle between them. Hence, the
second invitation is to the *intellectual* struggle surrounding what direction American foreign policy should take. This struggle is rooted
not in the distribution of policy-making powers and the dynamics of
politics, although this is where much of it plays out, but rather in the
unavoidable ambiguities, complexities, and uncertainties in thinking
about international politics generally and the substance of foreign
policy specifically.

Plan of the Book

The subtitle of this book could well be "Why is foreign policy so contentious?" or "Why do people disagree so much about foreign policy?"
It is organized to address these questions. The short answer is that foreign policy involves a series of tasks or questions related to identifying
and prioritizing interests, assessing threats, and evaluating policy options/
tools. Each of these tasks presents challenges that make consensus
difficult because the uncertainties, ambiguities, and value choices they
entail invariably provide fertile ground for reasonable people to reach
different yet perfectly plausible conclusions; hence, the invitation to
struggle. The bulk of this book explores these tasks in some detail in
separate chapters on each piece of what we can see as the foreign policy
puzzle—interests (Chapter 2), threats (Chapter 3), and tools (Chapter 4).
Each of these chapters discusses the major challenges, followed by two
brief case studies, one historical and another more contemporary, of
policies where disagreements about interests, threats, and tools were
central. The goal is to explain and illustrate why questions about interests, threats, and tools are so critical, why these questions are so difficult to address, and why these difficulties invariably fuel debates about
policy. These chapters are bracketed by two others. The first chapter
examines the debate surrounding the 2003 Iraq war with an eye toward
illustrating how a focus on conceptions of interests, assessments of
threats, and evaluations of policy tools/options helps us make sense of
policy and policy debates. The conclusion analyzes several competing
visions or grand strategies for the United States and how they bring the
pieces of the foreign policy puzzle together.

CHAPTER 1

Understanding the Iraq War Debate

The national debate surrounding the 2003 Iraq war was among the most consequential and contentious in U.S. history. A particularly striking aspect of the debate is how smart, knowledgeable, and sincere policy makers and analysts could arrive at such diametrically opposing conclusions. For the administration and its allies, the war to depose Saddam was one of necessity. The dangers of allowing him to remain in power and the benefits of removing him were great enough to justify a second war in less than three years. To critics and skeptics, who agreed with the administration on many points of fact (some of which turned out not to be fact), it was a rash and reckless war of choice built on imaginary and exaggerated fears. How could policy makers and analysts end up so at odds on an issue of such significance?

The general thesis of this book is that foreign policy is fundamentally about identifying interests, assessing threats, and evaluating/choosing tools. These are the basic intellectual challenges anyone thinking about foreign policy must confront. If this is so, we should also be able to make sense of the Iraq war debate by focusing on how supporters and opponents of war approached these issues. Disagreements about the wisdom of war should be rooted in more fundamental disagreements about the nature of U.S. interests, the magnitude of the threats to those interests, and/or the efficacy of various tools for protecting these interests given the threat. The purpose here is not to provide a comprehensive account of the debate. This is not a book about the Iraq war or any single foreign policy. Instead, the goal is to use this particularly important decision/debate to illustrate the utility, even necessity, of focusing interests, threats, and tools in thinking about foreign policy. There are certainly other examples that could have served the same function, many of which will be discussed in much less detail later. But is useful to begin with a somewhat in-depth analysis of a critical policy debate to fully appreciate how policy positions and debates are rooted in disagreements about interests, threats, and/or tools.

Background

In 1990 no one would have guessed that conflict with Iraq would come to define post–Cold War U.S. foreign policy, especially since the United States actually sided with Iraq in its war with Iran from 1980 to 1988. This was not out of any love for Saddam Hussein, of course, but because the new regime in Teheran was considered a greater threat to American interests in the region. As the old aphorism goes, the enemy of my enemy is my friend. In the wake of its Islamic revolution and the taking of American hostages, Iran became the new enemy and Iraq the new friend.[1] Many have forgotten that "during the late 1980s, President Ronald Reagan intervened in the Iran–Iraq War in support of Baghdad and Saddam Hussein."[2] Although it did not become involved militarily, the United States provided Iraq valuable intelligence. This came to an end with Iraq's surprising invasion and conquest of Kuwait in 1990, a move that altered the American strategic calculus in the region yet again, setting the two countries on a collision course that would ultimately lead to the 2003 invasion and all that followed.

In response to Iraq's seizure and brutal occupation of Kuwait, President George H. W. Bush and his secretary of state, James Baker, pulled together a broad international coalition to liberate Kuwait.

1. Shane Harris and Matthew W. Aid, "Exclusive: CIA Files Prove America Helped Saddam as He Gassed Iran," *Foreign Policy* (August 26, 2013). Accessed at http://www.foreignpolicy.com/articles/2013/08/25/secret_cia_files_prove_america_helped_saddam_as_he_gassed_iran/.

2. Bruce Riedel, "Lessons from America's First War with Iran," *The Fletcher Forum* (Summer 2013). Accessed at http://www.brookings.edu/research/articles/2013/05/lessons-america-first-war-iran-riedel/.

MAP 1.1 Iraq and Immediate Neighbors.

Despite fears of thousands of casualties, only 147 coalition soldiers were killed in the war. Although large and formidable on paper, the Iraqi military proved no match for American military technology and prowess. The coalition quickly expelled Iraqi forces but chose not to carry the war into Iraq to get rid of Saddam. President Bush and his national security adviser, Brent Scowcroft, later explained why: "Trying to eliminate Saddam, extending the ground war into an occupation of Iraq, would have violated our guideline about not changing objectives in midstream, engaging in 'mission creep,' and would have incurred incalculable human and political costs."[3] At the time, Colin Powell

3. George H. W. Bush and Brent Scowcroft, *A World Transformed* (New York: Knopf, 1998), p. 489.

agreed because "the Gulf War was a limited objective war. If it had not been, we would be ruling Baghdad today—at unpardonable expense in terms of money, lives lost and ruined regional relationships."[4]

Many were instead hopeful that Iraq's humiliating defeat would seal Saddam's fate from within, either by coup or by popular uprising. This was not to be. Saddam's grip on power proved too strong and his suppression of postwar uprisings was merciless. As the victorious President Bush went down to electoral defeat in 1992, Saddam survived. A decade-long low-grade war followed. Saddam's failure to comply with UN disarmament resolutions and obstruction of inspections led to the imposition of severe economic sanctions and occasional military strikes. Again, many hoped Saddam's days were numbered because they "quite reasonably assumed his regime could not last long in the face of his loss of Kuwait and heavy international economic sanctions."[5] When the sanctions "were initially imposed, most policymakers believed that Saddam Hussein would be the victim of a coup in short order."[6] But Saddam remained resilient and defiant, a constant thorn in the United States' side.

As Saddam played endless cat-and-mouse games with arms inspectors and his cronies continued to thrive despite sanctions that devastated ordinary Iraqis, many lost patience, urging the United States to get rid of him once and for all. These appeals did not fall on deaf ears and Saddam's removal became official U.S. policy with the Iraq Liberation Act (1998), which declared it "the policy of the United States to support efforts to remove the regime headed by Saddam Hussein from power in Iraq and to promote the emergence of a democratic government to replace that regime." It cautioned, however, that "nothing in this Act shall be construed to authorize or otherwise speak to the use of United States Armed Forces."[7] Passing the House of Representatives on a 360–38 vote and adopted in the Senate by unanimous consent, President Clinton signed the act into law. As the vote margins indicate,

---

4. Colin Powell, "U.S. Forces Challenges Ahead," *Foreign Affairs* (Winter 1992/3), p. 37.

5. Joshua Micah Marshall, "Bomb Saddam?" *Washington Monthly* (June 2002). Accessed at http://www.washingtonmonthly.com/features/2001/0206.marshall.html/.

6. Daniel Drezner, "Sanctions Sometimes Smart," *International Studies Review* (2011), p. 98.

7. The text of the act can be accessed at http://www.gpo.gov/fdsys/pkg/PLAW-105publ338/pdf/PLAW-105publ338.pdf/.

the goal of regime changed enjoyed nearly universal bipartisan support, even if the means for achieving it remained unspecified. It was only after the September 11 attacks and the initial phase of the war in Afghanistan that advocates of regime change saw an opportunity to go after Saddam. The result was one of the most significant debates in the history of American foreign policy.

Before looking more closely at the debate, however, we should recognize that many of those involved undoubtedly approached the question from both an intellectual and a political perspective. Their arguments almost certainly reflected genuine beliefs as well as political calculations about building support for/against war. The two are not always the same. The rationales policy makers find strategically compelling might not be the most politically persuasive. Participants in policy debates often act like lawyers in the sense that even if one piece of evidence should be sufficient to exonerate or convict, they are unlikely to rely on it alone in the courtroom. To earn an acquittal or conviction, lawyers present any and all evidence that might sway the jury. The lawyer's job is not only to prove guilt/innocence as matter of logic or evidence but also to convince and persuade those who control their client's fate. None of this is to suggest that anyone is "lying" (or that they are not). The point is simply that policy debates can, and perhaps inevitably do, reflect strategic analysis and political imperatives, and the two are often difficult to disentangle.

Interests

As is typical in foreign policy debates, the case for war was usually framed in terms of "national interests." Although the concept will be explored in more detail in the next chapter, here we can think about national interests by asking why Americans do or should care about something. In this case, why should it have mattered to Americans who ruled a country so far away? Saddam, after all, had already been in power almost a quarter of a century, so what was the harm of him remaining for another decade or two? Or, to flip the question, what benefits would flow from his removal? And was the harm and/or benefit sufficient to spend American treasure and spill American blood?

The crisis with Saddam did not emerge in a historical vacuum but rather as part of a long history of U.S. involvement in the Middle East stretching back half a century.[8] As a result, we should place the case for war against Iraq in 2003 within the larger framework of U.S. objectives/ interests in the region since World War II, because at least in some important respects it reflected a fairly traditional and widely accepted conception of American interests, although updated for the specifics of Iraq and Saddam Hussein as well as newer concerns about terrorism and weapons of mass destruction (WMD).

It was after war-weary, ravaged, and bankrupt European powers began to withdraw from the Middle East following two world wars that the United States became more actively involved their place. The region had taken on significance as a critical source of petroleum not only for the United States (which is fortunate to have substantial reserves of its own) but also, and perhaps more important, for the larger global economy. The objective of U.S. policy was to ensure that the oil continued to flow. To this end, the U.S. sought political "stability" in the region and the containment of hostile powers, whether they were external (e.g., the Soviet Union) or regional (e.g., Iran after 1979). Former secretaries of state Henry Kissinger and James Baker reflected this traditional view, arguing that the United States has "a vital interest in long-term stability in the Arabian/Persian Gulf, the source of much of the world's energy."[9]

The desire for stability and containment often led the United States to support governments whose character was difficult to square with its values of democracy and human rights. Hosni Mubarak in Egypt, the Shah of Iran (who was ousted in the 1979 Iranian revolution), the Saudi monarchy, and, perhaps most ironically, Saddam Hussein himself are prime examples. Within this general framework, the United States also maintained a commitment to the survival of Israel, a fellow democracy under almost constant siege from hostile neighbors and a succession of terrorist groups.

After the 1979 Iranian revolution, Islamic fundamentalism joined communism as a potentially destabilizing force in the region (recall that the Soviet Union invaded Afghanistan the same year). More recently, fear of Islamic fundamentalism has merged with heightened

---

8. A good introduction is Robert W. Stookey, *America and the Arab States: An Uneasy Encounter* (New York: Wiley, 1975).

9. Henry A. Kissinger, "Grounds for U.S. Military Intervention," *The Washington Post* (April 8, 2011). Accessed at http://www.washingtonpost.com/opinions/grounds-for-us-military-intervention/2011/04/07/AFDqX03C_story.html/.

concerns about movements and organizations with the ability and willingness to strike the United States in unconventional ways, as the September 11 attacks illustrated so vividly. So, in addition to more traditional objectives of stability and containing hostile states, there is a new focus on states harboring and/or supporting terrorist groups as well as the political and economic conditions in the region that make such organizations and their ideologies attractive. When we add to this already complicated mix fears about the proliferation of chemical, biological, and maybe even nuclear weapons, we get a good sense for the context of the Iraq war debate.

This returns us to the basic question of interests—why should Americans have cared about Saddam Hussein? The first response is that he controlled a potentially powerful country in a region long viewed as important for the reasons just discussed. In international politics, as in real estate, what often matters most is location, location, location, and Saddam's location was prime. He was, in President Bush's words, "trouble in his neighborhood," a neighborhood where the United States did not want "trouble." On this point there was little dissent. Opponents of the war did not think the United States could safely ignore Saddam or his neighborhood as unimportant. Indeed, there was substantial agreement about the nature of the interests at stake, and the administration articulated them clearly and forcefully.

The administration's brief for war weaved together a number of moral and strategic rationales. In terms of the former, administration officials seldom missed an opportunity to lace security-based arguments with moral outrage over Saddam's brutality. President Bush, for example, noted that under Saddam "tens of thousands of political opponents and ordinary citizens have been subjected to arbitrary arrest and imprisonment, summary execution, and torture by beating and burning, electric shock, starvation, mutilation, and rape. Wives are tortured in front of their husbands, children in the presence of their parents."[10] Although the administration never framed the war as a primarily humanitarian mission, it is easy to understand why these violations of human rights were highlighted so often. No doubt the revulsion and outrage were sincere given the despicable behavior of Saddam and

---

10. George Bush, "Address to the United Nations," September 2002. Accessed at http://georgewbush-whitehouse.archives.gov/news/releases/2002/09/20020912-1 .html/.

his sons (especially Qusay, whose penchant for torture and rape was legendary). Politically, of course, detailing the regime's depravity could only help build public support for war among those who preferred a moral justification instead of (or in addition to) a strategic rationale.

There was also talk of democratizing Iraq not merely to eliminate the threat Saddam posed but also as a first step in transforming the region by creating an alternative to the stifling political repression and economic stagnation terrorist groups and radical ideologies thrived on. President Bush held out hope that "a liberated Iraq can show the power of freedom to transform that vital region, by bringing hope and progress into the lives of millions." This was the only way to protect U.S. interests in the long term because "as long as that region is a place of tyranny and despair and anger, it will produce men and movements that threaten the safety of Americans and our friends." Consequently, "we seek the advance of democracy for the most practical of reasons: because democracies do not support terrorists or threaten the world with weapons of mass murder."[11] Condoleezza Rice, Bush's national security advisor and later secretary of state, echoed these sentiments in speaking of "a democratic Iraq, which can become a linchpin of a very different Middle East in which the ideologies of hate will not flourish."[12]

Despite such ambitious rhetoric, Rice did not place hopes of democratic transformation at the heart of the administration's case. A few months after the invasion, she sought to clarify the rationale for a war:

> Let us be very clear about why we went to war with Saddam Hussein. Saddam Hussein's regime posed a threat to the security of the United States and the world. This was a regime that pursued, had used and possessed weapons of mass destruction. He had links to terror, twice invaded other nations; defied the international community and seventeen UN resolutions for twelve years and gave every indication that he would never disarm and never comply with the just demands of the world. That threat could not be allowed to remain unaddressed.

---

11. George Bush, "Address on the Importance of Democracy in the Middle East," February 4, 2004. Accessed at http://georgewbush-whitehouse.archives.gov/news/releases/2004/02/20040204-4.html/.

12. Condolezza Rice, "Remarks on U.S. Foreign Policy," National Association of Black Journalists, August 7, 2003. Accessed at http://georgewbush-whitehouse.archives .gov/news/releases/2003/08/20030807-1.html/.

These were indeed the arguments the administration and its supporters hammered home relentlessly throughout 2002 and early 2003. Reflecting the traditional objective of containing hostile powers in the region, the arguments for war were presented against a background portrait of Saddam as a menace seeking to dominate the Arab world and control its vast oil wealth, an assessment usually validated by reference to Iraq's wars with Iran and Kuwait. Saddam was, in the words of Condoleezza Rice, "a man who has attacked his neighbors twice."[13] Secretary of Defense Donald Rumsfeld characterized Saddam as having "an attitude about himself that suggests that he wants to try to destabilize the neighboring countries, and periodically describes them as illegitimate, and attempts to take them over."[14] Vice President Richard (Dick) Cheney warned that if Saddam remained in power armed with WMD, "there is no doubt that his aggressive regional ambitions will lead him into future confrontations with his neighbors." And if he ever got his hands on nuclear weapons, "Saddam Hussein could then be expected to seek domination of the entire Middle East, take control of a great portion of the world's energy supplies."[15] Kenneth Pollack, one of the more articulate and influential analysts for war outside the administration, described Saddam as a "serial aggressor" with an "unparalleled record of aggression." Like Cheney, Pollack couched fears of Iraqi expansion in terms of the region's energy resources: "The strategic logic for invasion is compelling. It would eliminate the possibility that Saddam might rebuild his military or acquire nuclear weapons and thus threaten the security of the world's supply of oil."[16]

As Cheney and Pollack's arguments illustrate, the case for war combined traditional objectives of containing hostile states in the region with newer concerns about chemical/biological weapons and nuclear weapons. The synergy of the two was so alarming because WMD, particularly nuclear weapons, would make Iraq's neighbors, and maybe even the United States, less willing to confront and resist

---

13. Condolezza Rice interview with Wolf Blitzer, CNN, September 8, 2002. Accessed at http://transcripts.cnn.com/TRANSCRIPTS/0209/08/le.00.html/.

14. Interview with Donald Rumsfeld, CBS New Radio, November 12, 2002. Accessed at http://www.defense.gov/transcripts/transcript.aspx?transcriptid=3283/.

15. Dick Cheney, "Address to the Veterans of Foreign Wars," August 27, 2002. Accessed at http://www.theguardian.com/world/2002/aug/27/usa.iraq/.

16. Kenneth Pollack, "Next Stop Baghdad," *Foreign Affairs* (March–April 2002), pp. 36 and 43.

Saddam. As a result, the argument for war always returned to WMD. Human rights and democracy would appear from time to time, but the consistent theme was the need to eliminate Saddam's chemical and biological weapons and prevent him from acquiring nuclear weapons. When asked just days before the invasion in March 2003, "What do you think is the most important rationale for going to war with Iraq?" Cheney responded without hesitation, "Well, I think I've just given it, Tim [Russert], in terms of the combination of his development and use of chemical weapons, his development of biological weapons, his pursuit of nuclear weapons."[17]

Particular emphasis was placed on nuclear weapons. In a speech before the United Nations, President Bush stressed that

> Iraq continues to withhold important information about its nuclear program—weapons design, procurement logs, experiment data, an accounting of nuclear materials and documentation of foreign assistance. Iraq employs capable nuclear scientists and technicians. It retains physical infrastructure needed to build a nuclear weapon. Iraq has made several attempts to buy high-strength aluminum tubes used to enrich uranium for a nuclear weapon. Should Iraq acquire fissile material, it would be able to build a nuclear weapon within a year. And Iraq's state-controlled media has reported numerous meetings between Saddam Hussein and his nuclear scientists, leaving little doubt about his continued appetite for these weapons.[18]

Cheney sounded the same alarm, claiming, "We now know that Saddam has resumed his efforts to acquire nuclear weapons . . . many of us are convinced that Saddam will acquire nuclear weapons fairly soon. Just how soon, we cannot really gauge."[19] Debs and Montiero

17. Dick Cheney, Interview on *Meet the Press*, March 14, 2003. Cited at http://www.pbs.org/wgbh/pages/frontline/shows/truth/why/said.html

18. George Bush, "Address to the United Nations," September 2002.

19. Dick Cheney, "Address to the Veterans of Foreign Wars," August 27, 2002. Accessed at http://www.theguardian.com/world/2002/aug/27/usa.iraq/. The administration articulated no consistent judgment on how close Iraq might be to going nuclear. Although Cheney thought this might occur "fairly soon," Condoleezza Rice maintained "that left unchecked he [Saddam] might be able to have a nuclear weapon by the end of the decade, that's the judgment on which the president was going." But

argue that nuclear fears far outweighed other concerns: "The *main US motivation* for the war was to prevent suspected Iraqi nuclearization, which Washington thought would bring about a large and rapid shift in the balance of power in favor of Iraq . . . mak[ing] Saddam immune to any externally driven regime-change efforts."[20] Similarly, Pollack saw the consequences of a nuclear Iraq in nearly apocalyptic terms: "If Saddam Hussein is able to acquire nuclear weapons, he will see them as tools to achieve his goals—to dominate the Arab world, destroy Israel and punish America." [21]

Perhaps even more troubling, "in the aftermath of the [September 11] attacks, the Bush administration became particularly worried, based on flimsy intelligence, about the possibility of an Iraqi nuclear handoff to a terrorist group for use against US targets."[22] Cheney more than hinted at the possibility, claiming, "We know he's out trying once again to produce nuclear weapons and we know that he has a long-standing relationship with various terrorist groups, including the al-Qaeda organization."[23] President Bush himself drew the nuclear-terrorism link: "If the Iraqi regime is able to produce, buy, or steal an amount of highly enriched uranium a little larger than a single softball, it could have a nuclear weapon in less than a year. . . . And Saddam Hussein would be in a position to pass nuclear technology to terror-ists." "Facing clear evidence of peril," Bush concluded, with his vivid formulation of the potential danger, "we cannot wait for the final proof—the smoking gun—that could come in the form of a mushroom cloud."[24] Rice invoked the same imagery: "There will always be some

---

even the president sometimes suggested a much shorter time frame (see his reference to "less than a year" in the next paragraph). For the Rice comment, see http://www.pbs.org/newshour/bb/white_house-july-dec03-rice_7-30/.

20. Alexandre Debs and Nuno P. Monteiro, "Known Unknowns: Power Shifts, Uncertainty, and War," *International Organization*, (2014), pp. 16–17, emphasis added.

21. Kenneth Pollack, "Why Iraq Can't Be Deterred," *New York Times* (September 26, 2002). Accessed at http://www.nytimes.com/2002/09/26/opinion/why-iraq-can-t-be-deterred.html/.

22. Debs and Monteiro, "Known Unknowns: Power Shifts, Uncertainty, and War," p. 17.

23. Dick Cheney, Interview on *Meet the Press*, March 16, 2003.

24. George Bush, "Remarks on Iraq at the Cincinnati Museum of Art," October 7, 2002. Accessed at http://georgewbush-whitehouse.archives.gov/news/releases/2002/10/20021007-8.html/.

uncertainty about how quickly he can acquire nuclear weapons. But we don't want the smoking gun to be a mushroom cloud."[25]

It is difficult to know exactly what to make of these arguments. Returning to the observation that policy makers are often like lawyers trying to persuade the jury, it is possible that persistent references to terrorists with nuclear weapons provided by Saddam were intended mainly to alarm and scare the public into supporting war because, "from the White House's perspective, the war had to be sold to the American people in clear and simple terms."[26] One cannot imagine a much clearer or simpler danger than a 9/11-style attack with nuclear weapons. But was this simply a sales job exploiting vivid memories of that terrible day or a genuine fear, if one framed in particularly ominous terms? Unfortunately, there is no foolproof way to know. But unless one assumes that the public case for war was an elaborate smokescreen, it is difficult to disagree that "during the run-up to the invasion, the US government's *casus belli* rested on suspicion that Saddam was developing WMD—including nuclear weapons—thus presenting an imminent threat."[27]

The case for war was thus informed by a view of U.S. interests that included: (1) eliminating Saddam's WMD capabilities and programs, (2) preventing Saddam from using the WMD against his neighbors, the United States, or Israel, (3) ensuring that Saddam did not transfer WMD to terrorist organizations, and (4) containing his influence in the region. On these objectives there was little debate or dissent. To the extent there was disagreement, it was on nuances of prioritization. Some thought it was more important to focus on Afghanistan and pursue those directly responsible for the 9/11 attacks. Brent Scowcroft, the first President Bush's national security adviser, argued against war in 2002 as a distraction from more pressing tasks: "Our pre-eminent security priority is the war on terrorism, . . . [and] an attack on Iraq at

25. Condolezza Rice interview with Wolf Blitzer, CNN, September 8, 2002.

26. David Patrick Houghton, *Decision Point: Six Cases in U.S. Foreign Policy Decision Making* (Oxford: Oxford University Press, 2012), p. 225.

27. Debs and Monteiro, "Known Unknowns: Power Shifts, Uncertainty, and War," p. 16. Two good analyses of the administration's case and its treatment of the intelligence are Chiam Kaufman, "Threat Inflation and the Failure of the Marketplace of Ideas," *International Security* (Summer 2004), pp. 5–48; and James P. Pfiffner, "Did President Bush Mislead the Country in Its Arguments for War with Iraq?" *Presidential Studies Quarterly* (March 2004), pp. 25–46.

this time would seriously jeopardize, if not destroy, the global counter-terrorist campaign we have undertaken . . . any campaign against Iraq, whatever the strategy, cost and risks, is certain to divert us for some indefinite period from our war on terrorism."[28] Scowcroft held out the possibility that military action against Iraq might be warranted in the future, but in 2002–2003 the United States faced more important demands on its resources and attention.

Another way of looking at the issue of prioritization is to ask whether ridding Saddam of WMD was absolutely essential or merely desirable. There was little disagreement that the United States, its regional allies, and the Middle East as a whole would have been better off if he had no chemical/biological weapons and did not obtain nuclear weapons. The question was whether these objectives/interests were sufficiently important to take the step of going to war to achieve them. This is where the debate about war was joined in earnest. The answer to this question hinged on what Saddam was likely to do with the WMD he had and desired. This, in turn, depended on how Saddam was viewed—what kind of person was he and how did he make political/strategic calculations? This brings us to what may have been the critical disagreement driving the Iraq war debate—the nature and magnitude of the threat to the United States and its interests in the region, not the interests themselves.

The Threat

Amid disagreement about war, there were many points of agreement. No one denied that Saddam's regime was a loathsome and brutal tyranny. Everyone agreed that Saddam used chemical weapons against his own people and Iranians. No one denied that he had possessed and tested biological weapons. No one questioned that he sought nuclear weapons in the past and most likely still wanted them. In short, no one thought Saddam was a harmless leader with benign intentions toward his own people, the region, or the United States. Explaining his opposition to the war in 2002, Barack Obama (then still an Illinois State senator) conceded, "I suffer no illusions about Saddam Hussein. He is a brutal man. A ruthless man. A man who butchers his own people to

---

28. Brent Scowcroft, "Don't Attack Saddam," *Wall Street Journal* (August 15, 2001). Accessed at http://online.wsj.com/news/articles/SB1029371773228069195/.

secure his own power. He has repeatedly defied UN resolutions, thwarted UN inspection teams, developed chemical and biological weapons, and coveted nuclear capacity. He's a bad guy. The world, and the Iraqi people, would be better off without him."[29] Most opponents of war agreed with the future president.

There was also little disagreement that Saddam possessed a significant chemical weapons capability and maintained active chemical and biological weapons programs that he was trying to conceal. Although in retrospect there *should* have been more debate about this, at the time "there was a broad political consensus in Washington that Saddam possessed or intended to acquire WMD."[30] Although many U.S. allies opposed the war, "the belief that Iraq had active WMD programs was held by *all* intelligence services."[31] This is not to say that there were no disagreements. The state of Iraq's nuclear program, given the harsh sanctions in place, was a matter of some debate.[32] But in general, arguments about the war did not revolve around disagreements regarding Iraqi WMD capabilities and desires.

The question of why much of this proved to be so wrong is fascinating. One must wonder why Saddam behaved as if he had something to hide when apparently he did not. Why didn't he cooperate with weapons inspectors to have the economic sanctions lifted? Even if he did not care about the suffering of ordinary Iraqis, sanctions made it difficult for Saddam to rebuild the Iraqi military. Most likely, Saddam was engaged in a delicate high-wire act, hiding and revealing just as much as he thought was needed to manipulate the perceptions and calculations of domestic and international rivals:

> If it was made clear that Saddam had no chemical or biological weapons, then he would lose one of his key instruments of inflicting fear both among his own population and Iraq's neighbours. This

29. Barack Obama, "Speech on the Iraq War," October 2, 2002. Accessed at http://www.npr.org/templates/story/story.php?storyId=99591469/.

30. Debs and Montiero, "Known Unknowns: Power Shifts, Uncertainty and War," p. 20.

31. Robert Jervis, *Why Intelligence Fails: Lessons from the Iranian Revolution and the Iraq War* (Ithaca, NY: Cornell University Press, 2010), p. 134, emphasis in original.

32. See, for example, Alex Roberto Hybel and Justin Matthew Kaufman, *The Bush Administrations and Saddam Hussein: Deciding on Conflict* (New York: Palgrave, 2006), pp. 89–93.

could diminish Iraq's position as a major force in the region. Saddam's rational choice would then be to create uncertainty or ambiguity as to whether or not he actually had these weapons. Without proof of Iraq having WMD, it seemed unlikely that the West would intervene, and without proof of Iraq not having WMD, it would keep insurgents and Iraq's neighbours at bay.[33]

Why intelligence agencies failed to grasp this is an important question. It is, to be fair, difficult to get one's mind around the idea that someone is trying to hide the fact that they have nothing to hide. But this is an issue for another day. For our purposes, the more relevant point is that debates about the war were not rooted in disagreements about Iraqi WMD capabilities.

In thinking about why the consensus on capabilities did not translate into agreement on the need for war, we must recognize that an *ability* to do something does necessarily entail a *willingness* to do it. This is why the possession of WMD in and of itself is not sufficient to constitute a threat. France and Great Britain have several hundred nuclear weapons about which Americans do not worry at all. Russia and China have had nuclear weapons for decades and the United States has managed to live with it. No one calls for war to rid India of its nuclear weapons. The critical questions about such capabilities are always, Would they actually be used? If so, how and against whom? And could the United States prevent WMD from being used once acquired? These were the most contentious issues in debates about the Iraq war. And answers to these questions depended on how Saddam Hussein was viewed. Any judgment about what "Iraq" would do was essentially an assessment of Saddam. It is on this point—Saddam's likely behavior— that proponents and opponents of the war differed most sharply. This is why they disagreed about the level of danger Iraqi WMD posed and, thus, the need for war to eliminate them.

So what sort of leader was Saddam? Although there was universal agreement that Saddam was a repugnant goon, there was no consensus regarding his political and strategic decision-making style and

---

33. Tor Jakobsen, "Why Did the United States Invade Iraq in 2003?" *Popular Science* (November 25, 2012). Accessed June 2, 2014, at http://www.popularsoialscience .com/2012/10/25/why-did-the-united-states-invade-iraq-in-2003-2/. See also Kenneth Pollack, "Spies, Lies and Weapons: What Went Wrong?" *The Atlantic* (January– February 2004), pp. 78–92.

calculations. Hal Brands frames the issue well in asking, "Was Saddam an essentially pragmatic—if ruthless—statesman who operated according to calculations of power and security, or was he a delusional tyrant guided by innate aggressiveness, conspiracy thinking, and outsized visions of personal grandeur?"[34]

Although administration officials never offered a full psychological profile, their answer to Brands's question was clear. Discussing U.S. foreign policy generally after 9/11, President Bush, in a thinly veiled reference to Saddam, explained that "containment is not possible when *unbalanced* dictators with weapons of mass destruction can deliver those weapons on missiles or secretly provide them to terrorist allies."[35] Elsewhere, he was more direct regarding Saddam: "He's a man who a while ago was close to having a nuclear weapon. Imagine if this *madman* had a nuclear weapon."[36] Iraq was included in the category of "outlaw nations" that would use WMD to achieve their "mad ambitions."[37] And in his 2003 State of the Union address, Bush spoke of Saddam as "a brutal dictator with a history of *reckless* aggression."[38] Although hardly a sophisticated psychological analysis, "unbalanced," "madman," and "reckless" more than hinted at what the administration thought the United States was dealing with.

Pollack offered a more fully developed portrait, arguing that it was essential to disarm Saddam because "it is not at all clear that Saddam can be deterred successfully for very long." Why not? Why couldn't Saddam be deterred like Joseph Stalin, Nikita Khrushchev, or Mao Tse-Tung? Pollack did not think Saddam was crazy or a madman. Indeed, he cautioned that, despite his negative assessment, "this is not to argue that Saddam is irrational." To the contrary, "there is

---

34. Hal Brands, "Why Did Saddam Invade Iran? New Evidence on Motives, Complexity and the Israel Factor," *Journal of Military History* (July 2011), p. 862.

35. George Bush, "Address at West Point Graduation," June 1, 2002. Accessed at http://georgewbush-whitehouse.archives.gov/news/releases/2002/06/20020601-3.html/.

36. George Bush, "Remarks on Iraqi Disarmament," Souix Falls Convention Center, November 3, 2002. Accessed at http://georgewbush-whitehouse.archives.gov/news/releases/2002/11/20021103-3.html/.

37. George Bush, "State of the Union Address," January 29, 2002. Transcript at http://georgewbush-whitehouse.archives.gov/news/releases/2002/01/20020129-11.html/.

38. George Bush, "State of the Union Address," January 28, 2003. Accessed at http://whitehouse.georgewbush.org/news/2003/012803-SOTU.asp/.

considerable evidence that he weighs costs and benefits, follows a crude logic in determining how best to achieve his goals, understands deterrence, and has been deterred in the past."

Then what was the problem? Although not irrational, Saddam "has a number of pathologies that make deterring him unusually difficult." Opponents of war failed to recognize "that Mr. Hussein is often unintentionally suicidal—that is, he miscalculates his odds of success and frequently ignores the likelihood of catastrophic failure. Mr. Hussein is a risk-taker who plays dangerous games without realizing how dangerous they truly are. He is deeply ignorant of the outside world and surrounded by sycophants who tell him what he wants to hear."[39] Consequently, "it is thus impossible to predict the kind of calculations he would make . . . [and] leaving him free to acquire nuclear weapons and then hoping that in spite of his track record he can be deterred this time around is not the kind of social science experiment the United States government should be willing to run."[40] The policy implication of this image was clear—if Saddam could not be reliably deterred, he had to be disarmed. And if he refused to disarm, he had to be removed.

The danger was not only Saddam's use of WMD but also the possibility that he might hand them off to terrorist groups. This was the ultimate nightmare because, as Bush explained, "deterrence—the promise of massive retaliation against nations—means nothing against shadowy terrorist networks with no nation or citizens to defend."[41] With nations, deterrence is an option because they can be targeted and destroyed. No despot wants to rule over a radioactive ruin of a country. When it comes to nonstate actors, however, it is difficult to imagine how they could be deterred. The danger was that Saddam "would like nothing better than to hook-up with one of these shadowy terrorist networks like al-Qaeda, provide some weapons and training to them, let them come and do his dirty work, and we wouldn't be able to see his fingerprints on his action."[42] To preclude such a possibility, Saddam needed to disarm or be removed.

39. Kenneth Pollack, "Why Iraq Can't Be Deterred."
40. Pollack, "Next Stop Baghdad," p. 37.
41. George Bush, "Address at West Point Graduation," June 1, 2002.
42. George Bush, "Remarks on Iraqi Disarmament," Souix Falls Convention Center, November 3, 2002.

Opponents of war saw Saddam in a different, although certainly not positive or favorable, light. Contrary to the administration, they saw Saddam as an essentially rational calculator who valued one thing above all else—survival. Like Mao and other rogue leaders of the past, he was prone to rhetorical bluster and bravado. He was guilty of optimistic miscalculations in warfare. But rationality is no guarantee of always being correct, and miscalculation does not necessarily indicate irrationality (U.S. decision makers, after all, made their fair share of miscalculations). For war skeptics, the image of Saddam as a pathological, reckless, suicidal menace who could not be deterred and was anxious to hand off WMD to terrorist groups was a politically useful caricature based on a fundamental misreading of his behavior.

The notion, for example, that Iraq's war with Iran demonstrated reckless serial aggression was challenged as a gross oversimplification of the crisis between the two countries. Rather than picking on an innocent target, in 1980 Saddam was responding to a newly provocative, hostile, and threatening neighbor. Those who cited the war as an example of Saddam's "unparalleled aggression" had either forgotten (or did not find it useful to remind people) that in 1979–1980 Iran posed a threat to Iraq and the region in general. This was why the United States sided with and helped Iraq. The Ayatollah Khomeni was inciting the Shiite majority in Iraq to overthrow Saddam. Iran was shelling Iraqi towns along the border and attacking Iraqi ships.[43] From Saddam's perspective,

> Khomeni . . . was determined to extend his revolution across the Islamic world, starting with Iraq. By late 1979, Teheran was pushing the Kurdish and Shiite population to revolt and topple Saddam, and Iranian operatives were trying to assassinate senior Iraqi officials. . . . Facing this grave threat to his regime, but aware that Iran's military readiness had been temporarily disrupted by the revolution, Saddam launched a limited war against his bitter foe.

The war "was not a reckless adventure: it was an opportunistic response to significant threat." If it was a war of "serial aggression," it is one for which "Iraq received considerable outside support from other countries—including the United States."[44] Although the 1980–1988

---

43. See Brands, "Why Did Saddam Invade Iran?" pp. 865–866.
44. John Mearsheimer and Stephen Walt, "An Unnecessary War," *Foreign Policy* (January/February 2003), p. 53.

Iran–Iraq war was presented in 2002 as evidence of Saddam's uncontrollable and pathological aggression, this is certainly not how it was seen or portrayed at the time, even by the United States.

The 1990 invasion of Kuwait was another matter. Despite some Iraqi grievances relating to Kuwaiti oil production and the repayment of loans from the Iran–Iraq war, one can hardly characterize Saddam's invasion as a response to Kuwaiti provocation. But does one war a "serial" aggressor make? And even here critics saw little evidence of pathology, recklessness, and irrationality, only Saddam's typically cold and brutal calculation. He judged that Kuwait would be no match for the Iraqi military and that other countries, including the United States, would gradually accept his conquest of Kuwait as a fait accompli. Although he was wrong about the United States' reaction, it was not an unreasonable calculation. In August 1990 it was by no means certain that the United States would take military action to liberate Kuwait. The U.S. Senate, after all, only approved the use force by the narrow margin of 52–47. Saddam may have been just 3 Senate votes short of being right.

What about Saddam's use of WMD? There was no doubt that Saddam had used them. For the administration's critics the key point was that Saddam had only used WMD against targets that could not respond in kind. His own vulnerable citizens and the Iranians lacked the ability to punish him in return. In contrast, Saddam did not use chemical weapons against U.S. forces or Israel in 1991 despite his antipathy for the United States, his hostility toward Israel, and the prospect of an utterly humiliating military defeat. Taken in its totality, Saddam's behavior indicated that he would use WMD only against those unable to retaliate. His use of WMD demonstrated callous brutality, but his reluctance to use them against targets that could inflict substantial harm in return indicated a rational susceptibility to deterrence.

What about the possibility that Saddam would give WMD to terrorist organizations? Those opposed to war admitted that it would indeed be a disaster if he handed off WMD to al-Qaeda. At the same time, they noted that if Saddam were inclined to provide such weapons, he could have done so at any time over the previous two decades:

> Hussein has also refrained from giving or selling biological and chemical weapons to the Iranian and Palestinian terrorist groups that he supports. Radical terrorist groups—including al Qaeda—in

possession of such weapons and without a home address, could get the Iraqi government, which has a known location and a leader whose primary goal is survival, into a lot of trouble with the great powers. Saddam, ever paranoid, does not even let his own regular military units have biological and chemical weapons. So it is unlikely that he would give them to terrorists.[45]

The idea that Saddam would provide nuclear weapons to groups he had never armed with chemical or biological weapons was seen as even more improbable: "Saddam has been trying to acquire these weapons for over 20 years, at great cost and risk," and "is it likely he would turn around and give them away . . . [when] he would lose all control over when and where they would be used"?[46] One thing Saddam liked was control.

Thus, the debate over the war revealed two different images of Saddam and the threat he posed. Although supporters and opponents of the war alike viewed Saddam as a problem, a negative force in a volatile and important region, the question was how big a problem. To some he was, to use Colin Powell's famous description, a "toothache," an unwelcome but nonetheless manageable pain that recurred from time to time but required no major surgery. Others saw him as a malignant cancer, an existential danger to be excised even if it required radical surgery. These conflicting views were reflected in (and grew out of) divergent interpretations of Saddam's previous actions and entailed different predictions of how he was likely to behave in the future. These predictions were based not on Iraqi *capabilities* but on Saddam's *intentions and motivations*. And these conflicting images of Saddam and perceptions of the threat were important in evaluating war and deterrence as options for dealing with him.

Tools

Policy options can be evaluated along at least two dimensions—the likelihood they will achieve desired objectives and their costs relative to benefits. In the case of Saddam there were two main options on the

---

45. Ivan Eland, "Declassified CIA Report Undercuts Bush's Desire to Invade Iraq," *Cato Institute* (October 14, 2002). Accessed at http://www.cato.org/publications/commentary/declassified-cia-report-undercuts-bushs-desire-invade-iraq/.

46. Mearsheimer and Walt, "An Unnecessary War," p. 58.

table—deterrence and war. Evaluating the effectiveness of these options was closely related to assessments of Saddam. For the advocates of war, there was no effective alternative to Saddam's removal. Given his past behavior and decisional proclivities, the only way to make sure that he would not use or share WMD was to get rid of him. Critics agreed that the United States could remove Saddam by force, which would obviously prevent him from using or sharing WMD. War would be effective in this narrow sense. But it was not the only effective option. There was ample evidence that Saddam had been deterred in the past and could be in the future. With two options—war and deterrence—for achieving the same end, it was necessary to evaluate the costs associated with each option. If there are two potentially effective options, their relative costs became critical.

Early concerns about costs were evident in the debate surrounding how many troops would be needed to depose Saddam. The most fervent advocates of war within the administration insisted that it would require nothing like the half-million-strong multinational force deployed to the Gulf in 1991. A weakened Iraqi military combined with U.S. technological advances would allow a much smaller force to suffice. When Army Chief of Staff Eric Shinseki testified that the mission might require "something on the order of several hundred thousand soldiers," Rumsfeld immediately dismissed the figure as "far from the mark."[47] Shinseki made it clear that his estimate included securing the country in the aftermath of war, not just the requirements for defeating the Iraqi military and deposing Saddam. Although this was cast as a question of military needs, troop levels are related to costs. Committing several hundred thousand troops in expectation of demanding postwar stability and security operations suggested a lengthy, manpower-intensive, and challenging mission whose costs would be substantial.

The administration minimized the likely costs of war. Although admitting to uncertainty about how much resistance would be encountered, the general scenario assumed a fairly swift military victory with U.S. forces welcomed as liberators rather than occupiers. Saddam's defeat would be followed by a brief stabilization period during which a new, hopefully democratic, Iraqi government would be formed to guide the country forward. U.S. forces would then begin a phased withdrawal

---

47. Keith L. Shimko, *The Iraq Wars and America's Military Revolution* (Cambridge, UK: Cambridge University Press, 2010), pp. 144–145.

within a few months. This was not going to be a protracted and onerous exercise in "nation building." That would be left to the Iraqis, financed with the country's oil revenues and assistance from countries interested in a stable Iraq (even those who opposed the war itself).[48] Thus, war was the only effective option for dealing with Saddam and its costs would be quite modest. War would be effective and cost-effective.

Critics expressed doubts, seeing such a scenario as a wildly optimistic understatement of the likely costs. Christopher Layne was among those who suspected the costs of war would be much higher. Thanks to nearly two decades of war, sanctions, and a new war to remove Saddam, "the United States will inherit a mess . . . [and] America will 'own' postwar Iraq, and it will be America's responsibility to put the Iraqi Humpty-Dumpty back together again." This was unlikely to be cheap, and "wishful thinking of administration defenders notwithstanding, the Europeans are not likely to pay for cleaning up the mess caused by a war of which they did not approve."[49] Divisions within Iraq would complicate politics and governance after Saddam. As a group of prominent academics explained in a petition opposing the war, "Iraq is a deeply divided society that the United States would probably have to occupy and police for years to create a viable state."[50] The United States was simply not going to swoop in, oust Saddam, and then be on its way in matter of months. And beyond the direct costs of war and occupation, Layne feared strategic consequences, arguing that "war will destabilize the Middle East, which will lead to an upsurge of

---

48. Kenneth Pollack echoed the administration in arguing that "because it will be important to ensure that Iraq does not fall apart afterward, the United States will also need to repair much of the damage done to the Iraqi economy since Saddam's accession. It could undoubtedly raise substantial funds for this purpose from the GCC and perhaps some European and East Asian allies dependent on Persian Gulf oil. And as soon as Iraq's oil started flowing again, the country could contribute to its own future. Current estimates of the cost of rebuilding Iraq's economy, however, range from $50 billion to $150 billion, and that does not include repairing the damage from yet another major war. The United States should thus be prepared to contribute several billion dollars per year for as much as a decade to rebuild the country." "Next Stop Baghdad," p. 46.

49. Christopher Layne, "The Post-Saddam Quagmire: A View from the Right," *LA Weekly* (March 20, 2003). Accessed at http://www.laweekly.com/2003-03-27/news/the-post-saddam-quagmire/.

50. A copy can be found at http://mearsheimer.uchicago.edu/pdfs/P0012.pdf/.

terrorism. . . . the war will provoke freelance terrorism by 'amateurs' motivated by anti-American, pro-Islamic zeal."[51]

Layne's analysis reflected common concerns of many war skeptics. First, they thought the challenges of postwar Iraq were likely to be much greater, and thus more expensive, than the administration and its supporters maintained. Second, the hostility directed at the United States as a consequence of attacking and occupying another Muslim country at the same time it remained deeply entrenched in Afghanistan would undermine U.S. interests. Contrary to the administration's contention that regime change in Iraq was essential to winning the war on terror, critics worried that war would exacerbate the problem, enflaming anti-American passions and providing jihadists with yet another narrative of external domination for recruiting a new generation of radicals and terrorists. When all this was added to the equation, the cost and benefit columns seemed weighted decidedly in favor of the former, making deterrence the more cost-effective policy option.

Conclusion

More than a decade after the 2003 invasion of Iraq, the United States is still dealing with its aftermath, as it no doubt will for many years to come. Although errors in prewar intelligence and postinvasion implementation are widely recognized, some supporters, particularly administration officials, continue to argue that war was justified and essential. On balance, it left the United States and the region better off, even with all the errors and missteps taken into account. Others have recanted. Hillary Clinton, who voted for the war as a senator, eventually conceded in her memoir that although she "wasn't alone in getting it wrong . . . I still got it wrong. Plain and simple."[52] And as one might suspect, opponents of the war feel largely vindicated. Our purpose here, however, is not to judge the wisdom of going to war. The goal is simply to illustrate how focusing on interests, threats, and tools helps us understand the arguments for and against the war while clarifying and highlighting the underlying differences that fueled the debate before anyone knew how it would turn out.

---

51. Layne, "The Post-Saddam Quagmire."
52. Peter Beinart, "What's Missing from Hillary's Iraq Apology?" *The Atlantic* (June 9, 2014). Accessed at http://www.theatlantic.com/international/archive/2014/06/whats-missing-from-hillary-clintons-iraq-war-apology/372427/.

Although foreign policy debates are sometimes rooted in differences about U.S. interests, this was not the major point of contention in the Iraq war debate. The more fundamental disagreement concerned the nature of the threat—that is, whether Saddam was a brutal but nonetheless rational actor or a pathologically impulsive and aggressive despot. This was absolutely critical for evaluating the major policy options, particularly whether deterrence would be an effective alternative to war. This disagreement was compounded by differing assessments of costs, particularly the economic and strategic costs/consequences of war. For those who favored war, the main cost associated with a policy of deterrence was its possible failure: it provided no guarantee that Saddam would refrain from using or sharing WMD. This potential cost was simply too great to accept. But for those who preferred deterrence, the costs of war, although uncertain, were likely to be much greater than the optimistic scenarios suggested.

CHAPTER 2

....

Interests

Confident assertions about "the national interest" are virtually inescapable in discussions of foreign policy in which people are convinced that their policies advance whatever they think national interest is. The interests at stake are usually described as "vital" or some equivalent. References to anything other than national interests in general or vital interests in particular are rare. One seldom sees interests described as "secondary" or "peripheral." The identification of vital interests is almost a rhetorical requirement for entry into the realm of weighty foreign policy analysis and punditry. Some worry, however, that vital and similar adjectives are used with alarming ease and frequency. In the summer of 2011, for example, Stephen Walt, a Harvard political scientist and regular contributor to *Foreign Policy*, opened his email and found an announcement for a seminar on the United States' "critical" relationship with Kyrgyzstan. He could barely contain his incredulity:

> The idea that we have "critical" interests in Kyrgyzstan just illustrates the poverty of American strategic thinking these days . . . the central pathology of American strategic discourse is the notion that the entire friggin' world is a "vital" U.S. interest. . . . And Beltway briefings like this one just reinforce this mind-set by constantly hammering home the idea that we are terribly vulnerable to events in a far-flung countries a world away. I'm not saying that events in

Kyrgyzstan might not affect the safety and prosperity of Americans a tiny little bit, but the essence of strategy is setting priorities and distinguishing trivial stakes from the truly important. And somehow I just don't think Kyrgyzstan's fate merits words like "vital" or "critical."[1]

Putting aside the details of U.S.–Kyrgyzstani relations, Walt's frustrated rant about "pathologies" and the "poverty of American strategic thinking" highlights one of the more fundamental challenges in thinking about foreign policy—namely, identifying national interests and drawing distinctions between what's "truly important" and "trivial," vital and less than vital. This must be done before any evaluation of threats or policy options. We must know *what* is to be accomplished before asking *how* because "strategy must *begin . . . with purpose*; and purpose in foreign affairs strategy rests on a concept of the national interest."[2]

The "National Interest"

The national interest is "a ubiquitous term in the discourse of statesmen and scholars alike."[3] The concept is deployed so regularly that it is nearly impossible to imagine discussing foreign policy without it. What would remain, one wonders, of influential opinion journals such as *Foreign Affairs* if references to the national interest were purged and banned? Very little, one suspects. Would it be possible for a president to deliver a major foreign policy address that is not laced with references to the national interest? That is difficult to imagine.

Despite its ubiquity, the national interest is often seen as a deeply problematic concept. The mere fact that virtually any policy can and has been justified as being in the national interest suggests a degree of elasticity that for many casts doubt on the concept's value. This is all the more troubling because the national interest is sometimes invoked as if it is an objective thing. It is not. Conceptions of the national interest are just that, conceptions. They embody ideas and opinions, not

---

1. Stephen Walt, "Overcommitment Inc," *Foreign Policy* (June 30, 2011). Accessed at http://www.foreignpolicy.com/posts/2011/06/30/overcommitment_inc/.

2. Terry L. Deibel, *Foreign Affairs Strategy: Logic for American Statecraft* (Cambridge, UK: Cambridge University Press, 2007), p. 123, emphasis added.

3. Luke Glanville, "How Are We to Think about the 'National Interest?,'" *Australian Quarterly* (July–August 2005), p. 33.

facts susceptible to proof or disproof. As Stanley Hoffman notes, "the national interest is not a self-evident guide; it is construct."[4] Bernard Brodie made much the same point in his classic essay "Vital Interests: What Are They and Who Says So?" Despite "much glib talk about those [vital] interests, as if the speakers knew exactly what they are or ought to be," he reminds us that "they are not fixed by nature nor identifiable by any generally accepted standard of objective criteria." Vital interests (and national interests more generally) "are instead the product of fallible human judgment, on matters concerning which agreement within the nation is usually less than universal."[5] Arnold Wolfers addressed the same issue in analyzing "national security," a concept closely related to the national interest, as a highly "ambiguous symbol" whose meaning varies from person to person. Given this variability, "when political formulas such as 'national interest' or 'national security' gain popularity, they need to be scrutinized with particular care. . . . [because] they may not mean the same thing to different people . . . [and] might not have any precise meaning at all."[6]

No doubt Brodie and Wolfers are correct. In presidential debates candidates may reference the national interest without any guarantee that they are talking about the same thing. And in all too many cases, "statesman have been reluctant to define national interests with anything other than Delphic ambiguity."[7] But despite these well-recognized shortcomings, the notion of the national interest not only survives but also thrives. Even Wolfers only urged us to "scrutinize" these ambiguous symbols, not abandon them. The reason for the stubborn persistence of the national interest is not difficult to understand. Nations have foreign policies because their citizens are affected by what happens beyond their borders. People and governments are *interested* in what happens in the world because it matters to them for some reason. There is no better to term to convey this than the national interest, and any substitute would likely suffer from similar defects. Lack of consensus on what constitutes the national interest may be a problem if one is

---

4. Stanley Hoffman, "In Defense of Mother Theresa: Morality and Foreign Policy," *Foreign Affairs* (March/April 1996), p. 172.

5. Bernard Brodie, *War and Politics* (New York: Macmillan, 1973), p. 343.

6. Arnold Wolfers, "'National Security' as an Ambiguous Symbol," *Political Science Quarterly* (December 1952), p. 481.

7. James F. Miskel, "National Interests: Grand Purposes or Catchphrases," *Naval War College Review* (Autumn 2002), p. 96.

devising a theory of international politics, positing it as a central explanatory variable. But if the goal is to analyze issues and participate in foreign policy debates, the fact that the national interest "may not mean the same thing to different people" is precisely the point. This is perhaps the major reason we have debates about foreign policy—people enter into discussions of particular issues, problems, and crises with different conceptions, explicit or implicit, of what the national interest entails.

Thinking about National Interests

Joseph Nye thinks "there is nothing mysterious about the national interest." "It is," in his view, "simply the set of interests that are widely shared by Americans in their relations with the rest of the world. . . . In a democracy, the national interest is what a majority, after discussion and debate, decides are its legitimate long-run shared interests in relation to the outside world."[8] On one level Nye has a point. The conception of the national interest that ultimately informs American policy is determined through debate, discussion, and democratic processes that translate the preferences of citizens into policy. But on another level this is not a terribly helpful way to think about the national interest. The problem is self-evident. Someone who wants to participate in a policy debate can hardly wait to see what view of the national interest emerges from it. People must have an idea of the national interest during policy debates if they want to engage rather than just observe. And even after the debate ends, there is no obligation to accept the result. How the majority in a democracy defines the national interest is not binding or set in stone. It has changed before and it will again. There is no "after" when it comes to foreign policy debates. But for any of this to happen, people must think about the national interest apart from, and prior to, whatever conception eventually emerges from democratic debate and deliberation.

Most definitions of the national interest are sufficiently general as to be both unobjectionable and not particularly informative. According to one analyst, "in its simplest form, the national interest is the perceived needs and desires of one sovereign state in its relations with

8. Joseph Nye, "Why the Gulf War Served the National Interest," *The Atlantic* (July 1991), p. 54.

other sovereign states."[9] For another, it is "a finite set of intrinsically important goals either essential or beneficial to the country's survival, its prosperity, or the psychological well-being of its population, or any combination of these."[10] There are many such definitions, all minor variations on similar themes. But for the concept of the national interest to be useful, it must be unpacked a bit, initially in terms of *types* and *levels* of national interests, which we can frame as two questions. First, *why* do/should Americans care what happens elsewhere in the world? And second, *how much* do/should they care? The first question relates to *types of interests*, whereas the second deals with their *importance*.

Types of Interests

Americans care about what goes on beyond their borders for many reasons. They may worry that the spread of nuclear weapons to hostile states or China's increasing military power might eventually threaten the security of the United States. Such concerns are geopolitical and traditional, involving the types of issues that usually come to mind first when people think about foreign policy. There are also economic concerns. An economic crisis in Greece may appear distant as Americans watch violent clashes on the streets of Athens, but a collapse of the Eurozone could easily send European economies into a tailspin, which, in turn, could harm Americans whose jobs and well-being depend on exports to the continent. Beyond security and economic interests, there might be concerns about human rights abuses around the world. Whether it be the use of rape as an instrument of war, the torture of political prisoners, chemical attacks on defenseless civilians, or forcing children to serve as soldiers in brutal conflicts, moral outrages are upsetting even if there is no tangible harm to Americans because they are affronts to deeply held and widely shared notions of right and wrong.

None of this implies that we can always distinguish among strategic, economic, and humanitarian interests. Foreign policy often involves more than one type of interest simultaneously. A good example is the Marshall Plan in the late 1940s, when Europe was digging out

---

9. Donald E. Neuchterlein, "National Interests and Foreign Policy: A Conceptual Framework for Analysis and Decision-making," *British Journal of International Studies* (October 1976), p. 247.

10. Alan Tonelson, "The Real National Interest," *Foreign Policy* (Winter 1985–86), p. 49.

from under World War II's rubble and the Cold War with the Soviet Union was in its infancy. American policy makers judged that it was in the national interest to provide Europe with generous economic assistance to relieve hardship, rebuild ruined cities and infrastructure, and reconstruct the industries necessary for sustained growth and prosperity. What American interests did this serve? On one level, it had a significant, perhaps overwhelming, security rationale. The plan's authors believed economic prosperity was essential for stable political democracy and that democracy and prosperity were critical in countering Stalin's efforts to expand Soviet influence. Economic assistance was thus central to the United States' geopolitical strategy of containing Soviet communism. As the Marshall Plan's architects explained, "American effort in aid to Europe should be directed not to the combatting of communism as such but to the restoration of the economic health and vigor of European societies . . . not to combat communism but the economic maladjustment which makes European society vulnerable to exploitation by any and all totalitarian movements and which Russian communism is now exploiting."[11] In this case security objectives were pursued with economic means.

In addition to these clearly articulated security interests, a revitalized Europe was important for maintaining the economic prosperity most Americans experienced during the war, which was in sharp contrast to the decade-long misery of the Great Depression preceding it. The end of the war aroused fears of a return to the prewar depression if the rest of the world was unable to purchase American products once automobiles and appliances replaced bombers and tanks rolling off assembly lines. In this instance American security and economic interests coincided. A prosperous Europe could both purchase American goods and resist Soviet machinations. Finally, one can also see the Marshall Plan as a humanitarian effort to ease the suffering of people whose lives had been ravaged by war in countries toward which many Americans of European descent still felt a close affinity. Whatever the overriding motivation, the Marshall Plan simultaneously served American security, economic, and humanitarian interests.

This is not to suggest that the United States will always be so fortunate as to have its various interests converge. The point is simply that there are different reasons why Americans are interested in what

---

11. George F. Kennan, *Memoirs, 1925–1950* (Boston: Little, Brown, 1967), p. 336.

happens abroad. Sometimes these interests reinforce each other and point toward the same policies, as with the Marshall Plan. But there is no reason to assume that interests will always be in harmony, although making foreign policy would be a whole lot easier if they were. As in all facets of life, everything gets substantially more complicated and contentious when choices are required among things we value.

Prioritizing Interests

Walt's animated reaction to the briefing on Kyrgyzstan reflected his frustration with a common inability or unwillingness to distinguish what is vital from what is trivial. The announcement was a convenient foil for Walt to make the simple point that everything in the world is not equally important for the United States. This is partly just common sense. Is there anyone, for example, who doubts that a friendly government in Canada is more important than one in Paraguay or Tanzania? Could anyone disagree that commerce with China or Europe is more important than trade with Turkmenistan or Nepal?

In foreign policy, prioritizing interests is essential because national resources are limited. A country as populous, wealthy, and technologically advanced as the United States certainly has substantial resources. This is not in dispute. But even the United States' resources are not unlimited, and there are domestic claims on them as well as foreign. We must remember that "nations, even—especially—great powers, exist in a world of limited resources, where capabilities are never sufficient to exploit all opportunities and confront all threats." Consequently, "leaders must determine which interests are truly vital, which threats and opportunities are most urgent, and they must deploy resources accordingly." Even for the United States, foreign policy requires "ruthless prioritization."[12]

The notion that there is (or ought to be) a hierarchy of interests is not particularly controversial. There is little dissent on the general principle. It is difficult to imagine anyone arguing that everything is equally important or that the United States has sufficient resources to accomplish everything it might desire. The moment one concedes that some things are more important than others and resources are limited,

---

12. Brands, *What Good Is Grand Strategy?*, p. 4.

one has accepted in principle the need for a hierarchy of interests. But how is this general principle to be operationalized?

Since nearly everyone recognizes the need to prioritize interests, there is no shortage of schemes, rankings, and classifications. Hans Morgenthau, who played a major role in popularizing the concept of national interests, distinguished between those interests that were "indispensable" for the nation's survival and must be defended at "at all costs" and others that were merely "desirable," to be defended only under "favorable circumstances." He also differentiated "the *necessary* and *variable* elements of the national interest," the former involving "the survival of a political unit . . . the integrity of the nation's territory, of its political institutions, and of its culture."[13] More typical are frameworks distinguishing vital interests from a variety of lesser interests either lumped together or divided into series of subcategories. There is no logical limit to the degree of differentiation because "one can make as many gradations and subdivisions in the national interest as one wishes. . . . You could devise a 10-point or 20-point scale if you wished, but its precision [would be] spurious."[14] Most classifications use a small handful of categories.

In prioritizing interests, the crucial distinction is usually between those at the top of the hierarchy and whatever is right below. This is the fault line along which some of the most contentious foreign policy debates occur, largely because vital interests are presumably so important that virtually anything should be done protect them, including war, with all it entails in terms of the loss of life and treasure. In the allocation of scarce resources, one devotes whatever is necessary to protect/promote interests that are genuinely vital.

An entire book could be devoted to discussing various efforts to specify a hierarchy of interests. The goal here, however, is to illustrate, not catalog, to provide an example highlighting the challenges encountered in any such endeavor, particularly in terms distinguishing between vital and nonvital interests. A fairly thoughtful effort along these lines was provided by the Commission on America's National Interests, a somewhat politically diverse group of foreign and security policy

13. Hans Morgenthau, "Another 'Great Debate': The National Interest of the United States," *American Political Science Review* (December 1952), pp. 976–978.

14. Michael G. Roskin, "National Interest: From Abstraction to Reality," *Parameters* (Winter 1994), pp. 4–18.

luminaries. Formed well after the end of the Cold War but before the attacks of 9/11, the commission lamented the sense of drift that characterized American foreign policy in the absence of a Soviet threat. In the commission's view, the first step in crafting a coherent post–Cold War foreign policy was articulating a clear vision of American national interests independent of threats. The end of the Cold War had not altered American interests in the world, which are relatively enduring, only the nature and magnitude of the threats to these interests.[15]

The commission proposed a four-tier ranking. Not surprisingly, at the pinnacle were vital interests followed by "extremely important," "just important," and "less important or secondary" interests. *Vital interests* entail "conditions that are strictly necessary to safeguard and enhance Americans' survival and well-being in a free and secure nation."[16] Two elements of this definition stand out. The first is the qualifier "strictly necessary," a seemingly high bar narrowing the range of interests considered vital. Explaining that strictly necessary was designed to discourage "promiscuous" references to vital national interests, the commission, like Walt, was obviously concerned about interest inflation. It went so far as to claim that its use of vital was based "on the dictionary definition of the term: indispensible for survival."[17] The second element is the reference to the "survival *and well-being.*" Well-being in this context is nebulous, a vague term that could easily broaden the scope of vital interests beyond those strictly necessary for national survival. So although the commission sought to discourage conceptual promiscuity and interest inflation, the inclusion of well-being in addition to survival suggests something more expansive.

---

15. Graham Allison et al., *America's National Interests* (Harvard Belfer Center, 2000). Another framework that could have served the same purpose was provided by the United States Commission on National Security in *Seeking a National Strategy* (April 2000). This commission defined interests "at three levels: *survival interests*, without which America would cease to exist as we know it; *critical interests*, which are causally one step removed from survival interests; and *significant interests*, which importantly affect the global environment in which the United States must act. There are, of course, other national interests, though of lesser importance than those in the above three categories." The report can be accessed at http://govinfo.library.unt.edu/nssg/PhaseII.pdf/.

16. Ibid., p. 5.

17. Ibid., p. 14.

A step down in the hierarchy are *extremely important* interests, defined as "conditions that, if compromised, would severely prejudice but not strictly imperil the ability of the U.S. government to safeguard and enhance the well-being of Americans in a free and secure nation."[18] The difference between vital and extremely important interests lies in the formulation "severely prejudice but not strictly imperil," certainly a less demanding, if not terribly clear, standard. As the commission moved to identify these vital and extremely important interests, there were at least two obvious challenges. The first was differentiating conditions that would severely prejudice as opposed to strictly imperil the survival and well-being of Americans. The second was giving content to well-being in a manner that did not facilitate the conceptual promiscuity and interest inflation strictly necessary was supposed to prevent.

Pointing to some lack of clarity is not intended as criticism. Any conceptualization of interests at a general or abstract level will inevitably involve a measure of ambiguity. General conceptions must be translated into specific foreign policy goals. Thinking of vital interests in terms of conditions that would strictly imperil the survival and well-being of Americans is sensible enough. But what does this mean in concrete terms? What would strictly imperil the survival and well-being of Americans?

The commission's effort to translate abstract definitions of interests into specific goals can be found in Table 2.1. Although various hierarchies differ in how they rank and characterize interests, this is fairly typical. The commission identifies just five vital interests, which seems consistent with its desire for a somewhat restrictive, nonpromiscuous view of vital interests. Some are specific, narrow, and straightforward, whereas others are vague and broad. Preventing chemical, biological, or nuclear attacks on the United States or the emergence of hostile/failed states on U.S. borders (i.e., in Canada and Mexico) are self-explanatory interests. Both are narrowly focused and it is easy to see why they would be considered vital. If preventing an attack on the United States with WMD (or, presumably, conventional weapons) is not a vital interest, it is difficult to imagine what would be. Ensuring the "survival of U.S. allies," most of which are in Europe and Asia, reflects a commonly identified vital interest in assuring that no hostile power dominates/controls vast resources of Eurasia.

---

18. Ibid., p. 6.

TABLE 2.1 Summary of Interests

Vital U.S. national interests:
1. Prevent, deter, and reduce the threat of nuclear, biological, and chemical weapons attacks on the United States or its military forces abroad;
2. Ensure U.S. allies' survival and their active cooperation with the United States in shaping an international system in which we can thrive;
3. Prevent the emergence of hostile major powers or failed states on U.S. borders;
4. Ensure the viability and stability of major global systems (trade, financial markets, supplies of energy, and the environment); and
5. Establish productive relations, consistent with American national interests, with nations that could become strategic adversaries: China and Russia;
   Instrumentally, these vital interests will be enhanced and protected by promoting singular U.S. leadership, military and intelligence capabilities, credibility (including a reputation for adherence to clear U.S. commitments and even-handedness in dealing with other states), and strengthening critical international institutions— particularly the U.S. alliance system around the world.

Extremely important U.S. national interests:
1. Prevent, deter, and reduce the threat of the use of nuclear, biological, or chemical weapons anywhere;
2. Prevent the regional proliferation of WMD and delivery systems;
3. Promote the acceptance of international rules of law and mechanisms for resolving or managing disputes peacefully;
4. Prevent the emergence of a regional hegemon in important regions, especially the Persian Gulf;
5. Promote the well-being of U.S. allies and friends and protect them from external aggression;
6. Promote democracy, prosperity, and stability in the Western Hemisphere;
7. Prevent, manage, and, if possible at reasonable cost, end major conflicts in important geographic regions;
8. Maintain a lead in key military-related and other strategic technologies, particularly information systems;
9. Prevent massive, uncontrolled immigration across U.S. borders;
10. Suppress terrorism (especially state-sponsored terrorism), transnational crime, and drug trafficking; and
11. Prevent genocide.

There is more ambiguity regarding other vital interests, such as ensuring "the viability and stability of major global systems (trade, financial markets, supplies of energy, and the environment)." It is easy to imagine some questioning whether the stability of financial markets should be in the same category as preventing a nuclear attack. The stability of financial markets is probably not strictly necessary for the survival of the United States, but may be vital for the nation's economic well-being. The inclusion of stable financial markets, however, really begins to open up the range of interests deemed vital. So too does en-suring the stability of energy supplies, especially given the seemingly endless array of threats to stability in the Persian Gulf. One also won-ders why, if ensuring the stability of energy supplies is a vital interest, preventing a regional hegemon in the Persian Gulf is only a "very im-portant" interest.

The commission also added an addendum to its short list of vital interests highlighting things that, although they are not vital interests themselves, would nonetheless "enhance" the United States' ability to protect its vital interests. This is an interesting distinction. Perhaps most significant is the emphasis on "credibility (including a reputation for adherence to clear US commitments and even-handedness in deal-ing with other states)." For reasons discussed shortly, this has the po-tential to, at a minimum, complicate any effort to make and maintain a distinction between vital and lesser interests. If care is not taken, this addendum could completely undermine the commission's stated goal of identifying and prioritizing interests in a manner that discourages conceptual promiscuity.

As we move down into the much longer list of very important in-terests, similar points could made if each interest was examined and dissected in detail. Since our goal is neither to nitpick the commission's ranking to death nor to propose an alternative, an extended critique is not necessary. The lesson is simply that doing what almost everyone agrees must be done—identifying and prioritizing interests—is an in-herently challenging task. Perhaps this is why casual references to vital interests are so much more common than attempts to specify and dif-ferentiate them.

The Problem of Interest Inflation

Sometimes references to vital or critical interests should be taken with a grain of salt. Those who organized the briefing on U.S.–Kyrgyzstani relations that so riled Walt, for example, would probably concede that critical was a little rhetorical excess to cultivate interest. Trumpeting the secondary, peripheral, or less-than-vital issues at stake would have done little to boost attendance. It is highly unlikely anyone actually believed Kyrgyzstan was vital or critical. And in an official context, if a president regales a foreign dignitary by describing relations with her country as vital or critical, this may be more diplomatic nicety than

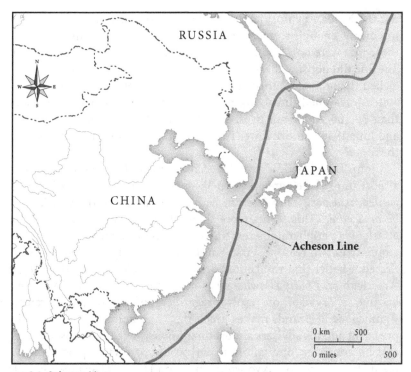

MAP 2.1 Acheson Line.

geopolitical analysis. Although some inflated rhetoric is easily ignored, the basic issue remains: foreign policy discussions are often characterized by interest inflation or, to frame it somewhat differently, an inability or unwillingness to consistently distinguish between vital and nonvital interests. And the problem is not just poor definitions or sloppy thinking. The very nature of foreign policy and the dynamics of international politics make this extremely difficult, and it is important to understand why and how seemingly nonvital interests often come to be regarded as vital.

There are few more vivid examples of these dynamics than U.S. policy toward Korea in the early 1950s. The "fall of China" to the communists in 1949 added a new wrinkle to American strategic calculations regarding the application of containment in Asia. In January 1950, the secretary of state, Dean Acheson, addressed the issue, specifying a defensive perimeter in Asia that included Japan and the Philippines but not the Korean peninsula, drawing a clear distinction between areas important enough to merit an American military commitment and those that were not. Japan and the Philippines were in; Korea was out. The line did not stay there long. When communists from the north attacked the noncommunist south a mere five months later, the United States intervened, involving itself in a three-year war costing more than 30,000 American lives. Why? What changed between January and June 1950 to move Korea from one side of the defense perimeter to the other?

John Lewis Gaddis explains that following the attack "there was almost immediate agreement in Washington that Korea, *hitherto regarded as a peripheral interest*, had by the nature of the attack on it *become vital.*" This seems more than a little curious. Why would an attack on a peripheral interest transform it into a vital interest? Gaddis emphasizes two reasons. First, South Korea's newly elevated status reflected a belief that the United States had to come to its defense "if American *credibility elsewhere* was not to be questioned." Korea thus became a "*symbol* of resolve regardless of its military-strategic significance."[19] Brands makes much the same point, noting that "the president and his advisers almost unanimously agreed, the psychological consequences [of a failure to act] would be catastrophic. Governments from Paris to Tokyo would question U.S. resolve; allied morale would suffer worldwide."[20] Second, Gaddis points to the warning offered by John Foster Dulles, Acheson's successor, that "to sit by while Korea is overrun by unprovoked armed attack. . . . would start [a] disastrous *chain of events* leading most probably to world war."[21] Thus, Korea was/became vital as a *symbol* of American credibility because of what *would/might happen* if the United States failed to act. Tellingly, neither rationale had much to do with Korea itself.

The Korean case is certainly remarkable for the rapidity and clarity with which the vital/peripheral interest distinction was erased, but the logics that caused its disappearance are by no means unique. So how did a peripheral interest become vital? References to "credibility," "chains of events," and "symbols" provide the answer. Each of these

---

19. John Lewis Gaddis, *Strategies of Containment* (Oxford: Oxford University Press, 1982), pp. 109–110, emphasis added.

20. Brands, *What Good Is Grand Strategy?*, p. 46.

21. Gaddis, *Strategies of Containment*, p. 110.

arguments entails placing Korea in a larger context, connecting it to something more important. Although Korea in and of itself might not be vital, the preservation of American credibility and demonstration of resolve is. And although the loss of Korea would not place American security in danger, it could have follow-on consequences that might. Although there is nothing inherently illegitimate about the underlying logic of these and similar arguments, we must understand how they complicate and undermine attempts to maintain a hierarchy of interests.

The argument Dulles and others made about a chain of events following a communist victory on the Korean peninsula is common in discussions of foreign policy. In trying to explain why great powers so often become embroiled in conflicts far from their shores where the stakes appear minimal, Michael Mandelbaum focuses on the "particular interconnectedness" of international politics in that "one thing can lead to another." "There is a propensity for international chain reactions to occur," even if "they are not inevitable." This made it reasonable for policy makers to think not only about whether the United States would be endangered by the loss of South Korea per se but also what other events this might lead to. Dulles thought the consequences would be dire, "most probably" world war. This was certainly debatable, but then any prediction about the consequences of action or inaction would be because such assessments are, by their very nature, "act[s] of imagination." Some might object to characterizing Dulles's judgment as an act of imagination since this conveys some sort of childish flight of fancy. But whatever term we choose—imagination, prediction, conjecture, expectation, or educated guess—the point remains the same: any chain of events argument rests on a *belief* about what *might* happen. As Mandelbaum explains, "the powerful send their forces abroad not so much because of what is occurring at the moment as in anticipation of the possible consequences."[22]

During the Cold War this chain reaction logic was evident in the famous "domino theory," suggesting that once one country "fell" to communism, a cascade would bring others tumbling down in a mechanistic and inevitable chain reaction. The only way to keep the last domino standing was to prevent the first from falling. The imperative

22. Michael Mandelbaum, *The Fate of Nations: The Search for National Security in the Nineteenth and Twentieth Centuries* (Cambridge, UK: Cambridge University Press, 1988), pp. 137 and 139.

was to prop up distant dominoes rather than wait until one fell on your doorstep. The logic of such arguments makes the first, perhaps distant, domino just as important as the last, more proximate domino.

A similar logic could be seen in Western Europe, whose overall importance was more obvious than Korea's. Although it never happened, American policy makers worried a great deal during the 1950s about a Soviet move on West Berlin, an isolated and vulnerable enclave completely surrounded by Soviet-controlled East Germany. There is little doubt the United States would have come to the defense of West Berlin. But why? If the Soviet Union had seized it, would this have strictly imperiled the survival of the United States? Probably not. After all, the United States survived quite well for decades with the rest of East Germany under Soviet control. What difference would half a city have made? It is difficult to argue that West Berlin per se was vital or "indispensible" to the United States.

This is not surprising. One can always cut things up into small enough pieces such that none of them on its own is vital. No one city or country in Western Europe was indispensable, but taken as whole they may have been. A Soviet move on West Berlin would not, and probably should not, have been viewed as a discrete event. West Berlin was part and parcel of West Germany, which in turn was part and parcel of Western Europe. A Soviet effort to control West Berlin would have been interpreted as an indication of aggressive and expansive ambitions in Europe, a prelude to more of the same better resisted sooner than later. This highlights the difficulty of pointing to any country, piece of territory, or issue that is vital in being something the United States absolutely could not survive without.

The potential analytical danger of always viewing interests in some larger context is obvious. Unchecked, this threatens to undermine efforts to distinguish peripheral from vital interests. It will almost always be possible to imagine a somewhat plausible chain of events in which a peripheral interest is connected to a vital interest, particularly if policy makers are inclined to rely on the worst *possible* chain of events. Of course, there is no reason the underlying logic must be taken to that extreme. But we must at least appreciate the central intellectual challenge or tension—recognizing the "interconnectedness" of international relations and the possibility of chain reactions while also maintaining a hierarchy of interests.

There is no easy formula for resolving this tension. Awareness of it, however, suggests a need to at least specify and scrutinize with great care any imagined chain of events, realizing that it is possible to err in either direction—minimizing or exaggerating potentially negative consequences. Whether thinking through policy yourself or analyzing someone else's position, the same sort of questions should be asked. What events/links are being assumed either explicitly or implicitly? How plausible or likely are the various links in the chain? One must be constantly on the lookout for assumptions slipped in as certainties, speculation masquerading as fact, and possibilities portrayed as inevitabilities. Returning to Dulles's warnings about Korea, for example, the issue is (or was) what specific events did he think would result from a communist victory in Korea that most probably would have led to world war? What was the roadmap from point A (the attack from northern Korea) to point B (world war)? Did it involve a sequence of events that was "individually imaginable, but collectively implausible"?[23]

Other logics pose similar dilemmas. As with fears of unfavorable chain reactions, concerns about credibility can also blur the lines between peripheral and vital interests. If the defense of a peripheral interest is necessary to establish or demonstrate the credibility of commitments to vital interests, as was argued in Korea, the distinction between the two may remain in theory but disappear in practice. In a chain of events logic, peripheral interests become vital via a sequence of possible consequences. With a credibility logic, peripheral interests become vital via their symbolic significance. In some senses, symbolic arguments are combined with an imagined chain of events—that is, predictions about how other states will interpret and respond to American action/inaction. When Gaddis noted with regard to Korea that policy makers worried about "American credibility elsewhere," he was referring to Western Europe. Policy makers thought (imagined) that one consequence of American inaction in Korea would be a more aggressive Soviet Union. Failure to act in Korea would lead Soviet leaders to question American resolve, creating doubts about the commitment to defend Western Europe. The defense of Seoul thus became essential for

23. Barry Posen, *Restraint: A New Foundation for U.S. Grand Strategy* (Ithaca, NY: Cornell University Press, 2014), p. 2.

the defense of West Berlin, although the two were thousands of miles apart.

Some are immediately skeptical of any argument resting on concerns about credibility, warning that "when credibility is the primary justification for action, it should be an indicator that the interest at stake is probably not vital to the United States."[24] Indeed, some research suggests that fears about a loss of credibility are easily exaggerated. Nations appear not to look to crises that are distant temporally or geographically to gauge their opponent's credibility. Much more important is whether they think the opponent has vital interests at stake in the crisis at hand. Soviet leaders would have realized that West Germany was more important for the United States than Korea or Vietnam.[25] The United States did not have to save Seoul or Saigon to prove that its commitment to Berlin was real. Nonetheless, the credibility argument remains intuitively appealing.

In principle, there is widespread agreement that prioritizing interests is an essential element of strategy. This entails drawing lines between what is trivial, what is vital, and everything in between. Acheson's defense perimeter was one attempt to do so. It was literally a line on the map representing a hierarchy of interests. It did not last long. We can see similar line drawing in the commission's attempt to differentiate vital from lesser interests. Preventing "the emergence of hostile major powers or failed states *on U.S. borders*," for example, is identified as a vital interest, implying that preventing the emergence of a hostile major power or failed states anywhere other than Mexico or Canada is *not* a vital interest. But one can easily see how this line might give way, like Acheson's defense perimeter. What about a hostile power or failed state on the border of a critical ally? What about a more distant failed state that becomes a base for terrorist organizations to launch attacks on the United States? After all, those who planned and launched the 9/11 attacks were in Afghanistan, about as far from U.S. borders as possible. Since threats can emanate from distant lands, why is it not a vital interest to prevent failed states anywhere?

---

24. Christopher Fettweis, *The Pathologies of Power: Fear, Honor, Glory and Hubris in U.S. Foreign Policy* (Cambridge, UK: Cambridge University Press, 2013), p. 112.

25. See Daryl G. Press, *Calculating Credibility: How Leaders Assess Military Threats* (Ithaca, NY: Cornell University Press, 2007).

Again, the point is not to be critical but rather to illustrate how and why drawing lines, literal or figurative, that reflect a hierarchy of interests is so inherently problematic. And even when we can do so on paper, in the real world policy makers are often confronted with challenges to less-than-vital interests that are difficult to analyze in isolation. Fears of chain reactions and losing credibility are among the reasons why. They are not the only ones. There are many variants on the same basic theme of peripheral interests being connected to vital interests. The intellectual dilemma would be easier to deal with if such concerns were baseless. But they are not that easy to dismiss. Thus, constant intellectual vigilance is required to simultaneously recognize and appreciate such concerns without allowing them to eclipse a central task of strategy—determining what objectives/interests are more important and allocating resources accordingly.

Values and Interests

This discussion of interests might seem like another manifestation of what Zach Beauchamp characterizes as "the toxic cult of America's national interest . . . [that] worships at the altar of American selfishness."[26] It is probably more accurate to say that it has thus far dodged the issue of whether the national interest should be the basis, or at least the sole basis, for American foreign policy. We began this chapter with the observation that "purpose in foreign affairs strategy rests on a concept of the national interest." The question is whether national interests should be *part* of that purpose or its totality. Beauchamp does not deny the existence of national interests. He merely rejects the proposition that these interests should be the nation's only guide. This leads to the next critical question: if we think about foreign policy in terms of interests, where and how should moral and humanitarian concerns enter the equation? If, for example, a brutal civil war or egregious violation of human rights on the other side of the world has no impact on the nation's security or the well-being of its citizens, is no national interest at stake? And if there is no national interest, should the United States be indifferent? Or should moral values also shape policy? And to further complicate matters, what should be done if moral values conflict with

26. Zack Beauchamp, "The Toxic Cult of America's National Interest," *The Week* (January 23, 2014). Accessed at http://theweek.com/article/index/255436/the-toxic-cult-of-americas-national-interest/.

security or economic interests? The Commission on National Interests' treatment of genocide highlights the dilemmas involved in such questions. But before we deal with that, it useful to examine how others, including the "toxic cult" Beauchamp lambasts, wrestle with the enduring questions of morality in foreign policy.

A Harmony of Interests and Values?

Many questions about morality in foreign policy assume there is sometimes a conflict or tension between the protection of interests and fidelity to values. If the two were always in alignment, there would be no dilemma. Difficulties arise in two scenarios. The first is when protecting interests requires policies that conflict with the nation's values, such as supporting nondemocratic, authoritarian, and highly repressive regimes during the Cold War in pursuit of "stability" or out of fear that more representative governments would be hostile to American interests. The second scenario is when there is a strong moral case for action without any apparent, tangible interest. In the first scenario the dilemma is the choice between interests and moral values, whereas in the second it is whether to act on moral values alone.

Some resolve these dilemmas by essentially denying their existence. In terms of the first scenario, they claim there are few, if any, instances in which the United States must go against its values to protect its interests. The United States did not, for example, have to support repressive regimes during the Cold War. The fact that it did has come back to haunt it in places like Egypt, where the United States is now associated with the corruption and repression of leaders it supported for decades. Anti-Americanism in these places is so deeply entrenched because previous policies were inconsistent with American values. If the United States had encouraged reform and democracy in the past, its interests would be more secure today. As a result, "American foreign policy should be informed with a clear moral purpose, based on the understanding that its moral goals and fundamental national interests are almost always in harmony."[27] If morality and interests are "almost always" in harmony, there is no need to choose.

---

27. William Kristol and Robert Kagan, "Toward a Neo-Reaganite Foreign Policy," *Foreign Affairs* (July/August 1996), p. 27.

In scenarios where there is a moral case for action but no obvious interest, we are urged to look harder for the national interests too often overlooked. Stanley Hoffman expressed this perspective best:

> We live in a world in which apathy about what happens in "far away countries of which we know nothing" can all too easily lead— through contagion, through the message such moral passivity sends to troublemakers, would-be tyrants, and ethnic cleaners elsewhere— not to the kind of Armageddon we feared during the Cold War but to a creeping escalation of disorder and beastliness that will, sooner or later, reach the shores of the complacent, the rich, and the indifferent.[28]

Here we have another variant of a chain reaction logic in which remote atrocities that appear to have no impact will have follow-on and cumulative consequences undermining an international order in which Americans can feel secure and content. This eliminates the dilemma of acting in the absence of a national interest by asserting that there actually is a national interest despite superficial appearances to the contrary.

Not everyone, however, is convinced that conflict between American interests and values is so rare. Christopher Caldwell sees this "faith that one's interests are always in harmony with one's principles" as an almost uniquely "American failing." He points to the dilemmas of the Arab Spring in 2011 as the most recent example. As popular movements ousted authoritarian leaders long supported by the United States as stabilizing forces throughout the region, he thought American principles would be put to the test, especially in Egypt, where greater democracy would undoubtedly produce a government more hostile to the United States and its ally, Israel. Although "Presidents George W. Bush and Barack Obama have made it a priority to sow democracy in the Middle East. . . . The question facing Mr. Obama is whether the US should support democracy even when it is against US interests."[29] Some might contend that the United States is only in this predicament because it failed to follow it principles in the past. Perhaps so, although we cannot know how different policies would have played out. Some insist,

---

28. Hoffman, "In Defense of Mother Theresa: Morality and Foreign Policy," p. 175.

29. Christopher Caldwell, "America's Principles Clash with Its Interests," *Financial Times* (February 4, 2011). Accessed at http://www.ft.com/intl/cms/s/0/9b2c8f92-3095-11e0-9de3-00144feabdc0.html#axzz3Kss5O7kb/.

however, that the United States cannot always count on the happy co-incidence of interests and values. Considering U.S. options in Syria, for example, Chase Carter concludes, "American idealism frequently clouds the judgment of our policy makers. We want to promote democracy everywhere, and we have a seemingly nonnegotiable aversion to dictators. But sometimes there simply isn't a better alternative."[30]

Interests over Values

Interestingly, although there is disagreement about how frequently a choice must be made between interests and values, few think the choice can always be avoided. Even if American interests and values are "almost always in harmony," almost always is not always. Whether policy makers are confronted with the dilemma rarely or often, they must think about the choice.

For foreign policy realists, many of whom belong to Beauchamp's toxic cult, the answer is clear—the national interest should prevail. This perspective was reflected vividly in Samuel Huntington's objection to the U.S. intervention in Somalia in 1992, which is "the only instance during the past one hundred years in which U.S. soldiers were killed in action on a humanitarian mission."[31] Most are familiar with the Somali experience through the movie *Blackhawk Down* and its climatic scene where a helicopter is shot down in Mogadishu and the charred remains of American soldiers are dragged through the streets as locals look on and jeer. The real incident signaled the beginning of the end of American involvement in Somalia. But even before the intervention's messy end, Huntington was positively livid, fuming that "it is morally unjustifiable and politically indefensible that members of the [U.S.] armed forces should be killed to prevent Somalis from killing each other."[32] Why was this "morally unjustifiable?" Because the primary moral obligation of the American government is protecting the security and well-being of *Americans*, not Somalis. To put the lives of

30. Chase Carter, "The Case for Assad," *The National Interest* (June 20, 2014). Accessed at http://nationalinterest.org/feature/the-case-assad-10708/.

31. John Mearsheimer, *The Tragedy of Great Power Politics* (New York: Norton, 2001), p. 47.

32. Michael J. Smith, "Humanitarian Intervention: An Overview of Ethical Issues," *Ethics and International Affairs* 12 (1998), p. 63.

Americans in danger to protect the lives of Somalis was an unacceptable negation of this obligation.

George Kennan espoused this position in somewhat less inflammatory terms in a famous essay, "Morality and Foreign Policy," in which he differentiated individual from state morality. If I as an individual place myself in harm's way to promote my moral values, I should be free to do so because I am placing only myself in danger. But if a president sends Americans to Somalia, this is problematic because he is placing at risk people he is obligated to protect. Kennan drew an analogy between governments and lawyers: "No more than the attorney vis-à-vis the client . . . can government attempt to insert itself into the consciences of those whose interests it represents."[33] Just as lawyers are hired to jealously and selfishly protect their clients' interests, governments are "hired" to defend the interests of their citizens, not others.

This position continues to resonate with realists. Damon Linker echoes the sentiment in thinking about intervention in places like Syria. "Duties to expiate sins and render aid apply to people, not to states. As a private individual, Barack Obama can have a moral duty to come to the aid of a person under attack," but as "president of the United States . . . his singular, overarching duty is a political one—namely, to protect and defend our nation and its citizens. Not any other nation. Not any other citizens."[34] Here Linker points to the fundamental question: Is protecting the nation and its citizens the *singular* duty of American policy makers? The issue is "whether you believe the United States has moral obligations to foreigners, and at what point you believe those duties can trump America's obligations to its own citizens."[35]

Duties beyond Borders[36]

The counter is that there are indeed moral obligations extending beyond a nation's borders or a government's own citizens. Although

33. Ibid.

34. Damon Linker, "The Danger of Injecting Morality into Foreign Policy," *The Week* (January 27, 2014). Accessed at http://theweek.com/article/index/255558/the-danger-of-injecting-moralism-into-foreign-policy/.

35. Beauchamp, "The Toxic Cult of America's National Interest."

36. This is taken from Stanley Hoffman, *Duties beyond Borders: On the Limits and Possibilities of Ethical International Politics* (Syracuse, NY: Syracuse University Press, 1981.)

Hoffman, for example, tried his best to frame responses to distant moral outrages in national interest terms (i.e., the cumulative break down in order would eventually bring danger close to home), he ultimately rejects the need to make a national interest case for action. In the final analysis, he really does not care "whether it is our 'interest' to intervene to stop genocide or war crimes on a colossal scale." This is a question for "the sophists of national security [to] argue among themselves." Regardless of their answer, Hoffman wants the United States to do something because it "is our moral duty to act, whenever there is chance of success."[37] Despite his attempt to offer a national interest rationale, Hoffman is comfortable calling for action without it. In this view, moral obligations independent of interests are a legitimate element of American foreign policy. Morality can enter the policy equation directly. It need not be smuggled in under the guise of interests.

With this background, it is interesting to see how the Commission on National Interests dealt with genocide. It ranks the prevention of genocide as an extremely important, not a vital, interest. Aware that many would wonder why, the commission offered a preemptive explanation:

> More controversial, we suspect, will be this Commission's unwillingness to consider "preventing genocide" or "preventing the use of nuclear, biological, or chemical weapons anywhere" as vital national interests for the United States. But when we ask ourselves whether prevention of genocide in Rwanda (as occurred in 1994) or Burundi (as may occur this year or next) or the use of nuclear weapons between India and Pakistan (as may occur in the years immediately ahead) is strictly necessary for the United States to survive as a free nation with our fundamental institutions and values intact, we believe the answer is clear. Such atrocities are horrific and should be prevented. If they occur, they will have serious consequences for Americans' well-being in a free and secure nation. They do not, however, strictly imperil the ability of the US government to safeguard and enhance US survival and freedom, and thus are "extremely important" in our hierarchy.[38]

The commission did indeed strictly adhere to its definition in refusing to classify the prevention as a vital interest. Although the commission

---

37. Hoffman, "In Defense of Mother Theresa: Morality and Foreign Policy," p. 175.
38. Allison et al., *America's National Interests*, p. 20.

justifies the prevention's exclusion from the realm of vital interests, no explanation is offered as to why it is an extremely important interest. Recall the commission's definition of extremely important interests as "conditions that, if compromised, would *severely prejudice* but not strictly imperil the ability of the US government to safeguard and enhance the well-being of Americans in a free and secure nation." The commission argues persuasively that a distant genocide would not strictly imperil the United States, but fails to explain how it would severely prejudice the security and well-being of Americans.

Regrettably, these issues are not abstract or hypothetical. Over the course of eight weeks in 1994, an estimated 800,000 Rwandan Tutsis perished in grisly fashion at the hands of their Hutu countrymen, a rate of killing probably unparalleled in history. Despite handwringing and expressions of regret after the fact, nothing of consequence was done to halt the bloodbath.[39] There can be no doubt the Rwandan genocide was a moral catastrophe of the highest order. But in terms of the commission's framework, what precisely were its serious consequences for the United States? How did it severely prejudice the security and well-being of Americans? The United States obviously survived the Rwandan genocide "as a free nation with our fundamental institutions and values intact." How was the security or well-being of Americans endangered even slightly? This might seem like an extremely callous question in light of such carnage, but it is unavoidable given the commission's determination to be hard-headed in applying its hierarchy of interests in a manner that discourages interest inflation. In fact, it is difficult to see how preventing genocide flows from the definition of extremely important interests the commission itself provided. Thus, we appear to have a specific foreign policy goal classified as extremely important for reasons that are neither obvious nor explained.

It is difficult to avoid the conclusion that a moral imperative led the commission to view the prevention of genocide as a high, if not the highest, priority, but it was determined to cast it as a national interest rather than as a moral obligation, requiring some assertion of serious consequences that would severely prejudice the security and well-being of Americans. Unlike Hoffman, the commission was unwilling to prioritize a foreign policy objective on the basis of morality alone and thus

---

39. See Michael Barnet, *Eyewitness to Genocide: The United Nations and Rwanda* (Ithaca, NY: Cornell University Press, 2003).

incorporated it as a national interest by citing unspecified serious consequences. Perhaps Peter Beinart is on the right track in arguing that "at times, the politicians or pundits might admit that Americans have no tangible interests in a given country, just a moral obligation to prevent killing, poverty, or oppression. That'd be fine. At least they'd be making their case honestly."[40]

Conclusion

In a critique of President Obama's foreign policy, particularly his response to the Islamic State, Rosa Brooks offers the fairly common advice that the United States "should intervene militarily to clean up short-term global messes only when doing so is *essential* to protecting our *core* interests."[41] This is the sort of recommendation with which almost everyone nods in agreement. It recognizes that not everything is equally important and that there is a hierarchy of interests. But the universal agreement is partly the result of vagueness and generality. The proposition that military force should be used only in the defense of core/vital interests is the motherhood and apple pie of foreign policy strategy, something difficult to disagree with. Unfortunately, it does not get us far in thinking about foreign policy because it begs the most important and contentious questions. Most obviously, what exactly are the nation's core interests? How narrowly or broadly should they be defined? As these more pointed and difficult questions are asked and answered, the nods of approval give way to argument and debate.

Even if core interests are specified in manner clearly distinguishing them from lesser interests, this is only part of the challenge. In practice, the distinction is often difficult to sustain because it is easy to imagine how threats to lesser interests could eventually endanger core/vital interests. The result is a strong temptation—and perhaps good arguments— for action before core interests are threatened. The Islamic State, for example, might not have threated core U.S. interests when military action against it began in the fall of 2014, but one could see how it *might* eventually if left unchecked. Although the Islamic State could have failed

---

40. Peter Beinart, "Putting Ukraine in Its Place," *The Atlantic* (June 2014). Accessed at http://www.theatlantic.com/magazine/archive/2014/06/putting-ukraine-in-its-place/361627/.

41. Rosa Brooks, "Embrace the Chaos," *Foreign Policy* (November 14, 2014). Accessed at http://foreignpolicy.com/2014/11/14/embrace-the-chaos/.

for other reasons long before that, there was no way to know at the time. Thus, should the United States have waited to see whether a threat to its core interests materialized or was it wiser to combat the emerging threat well in advance? Such questions return us to the central dilemma of recognizing and appreciating the interconnectedness of international politics while maintaining a hierarchy of interests in both in theory and in practice.

DEBATING INTERESTS, PAST AND PRESENT

Past: Vietnam

If actions taken and costs incurred were commensurate with stakes and interests, one might be forgiven for thinking Vietnam was one of the most strategically important places on earth. It was in this corner of Southeast Asia that the most powerful country the world has ever known waged war for more than a decade at great cost in treasure and lives to preserve an independent and noncommunist South Vietnam. Although U.S. aid and assistance remained modest through much of the late 1950s and early 1960s, the escalation of the mid-1960s was dramatic. Hixson highlights the sheer scale of the United States' involvement, almost marveling that "by 1967 gargantuan B-52 bombers had rained more bombs on Vietnam than had been dropped in all theaters of World War II."[42] Even then, it was still six more years until the war reached its ragged end with more than 50,000 U.S. soldiers killed. By 1975 South Vietnam had "fallen," an outcome Americans had been warned through-out their ordeal would be catastrophic in the global struggle against communism.

Although U.S. sacrifices defending South Vietnam would suggest it was strategically critical, that the United States nonetheless prevailed in the Cold War just fifteen years later is prima facie evidence that it really was not. Whatever the consequences for the Vietnamese, neither the security of the United States nor its prospects in the Cold War seemed to suffer. Communist victory in Vietnam may have been regrettable on many levels, but for the United States at least it was obviously not calami-tous. But this became clear only in retrospect. At the time, many thought the consequences of defeat would be dire. One does not send tens of thousands of soldiers to their deaths for anything that is not vital. But why exactly was the fate of South Vietnam, a poor and distant country of ap-proximately 15 million, deemed so important?

Of course, no one really argued that South Vietnam per se was abso-lutely critical for U.S. security and survival. How it aligned in the Cold War would not exactly have shifted the distribution of power in any decisive way. Although it does have a long coast on the strategically important South China Sea, this was seldom mentioned in arguments for the war. The primary rationale was laid out numerous times in both private and

---

42. Walter L. Hixson, *George F. Kennan: Cold War Iconoclast* (New York: Columbia University Press, 1991), p. 232.

MAP **2.2 Southeast Asia.**

public. A 1963 National Security Action Memorandum leaked and published as part of the *Pentagon Papers* is representative:

> We seek an independent and non-Communist South Vietnam . . . unless we can achieve this objective in South Vietnam, almost all of Southeast Asia will probably fall under Communist dominance . . . Thailand might hold for a period without help, but would be under grave pressure. Even the Philippines would become shaky, and the threat to India on the West, Australia and New Zealand to the South, and Taiwan, Korea and Japan to the North and East would be greatly increased.[43]

---

43. Leslie Gelb (with Richard Betts), *The Irony of Vietnam: The System Worked* (Washington D.C.: The Brookings Institution, 1979), p. 187.

continued

continued

This is quintessential domino theory, linking the fate of an apparently nonvital country to the security of countries more easily seen as important: Vietnam itself might not be vital, but surely Japan and Australia were. If a communist victory in South Vietnam would not only doom all of Southeast Asia but also "greatly increase" the threat to these allies, all of Asia and Oceania would be in danger. Similarly, Senator Milton Young (R-ND) warned that "if the communist-led Viet Cong movement in South Vietnam succeeds, there is little to stop the communists from spreading West and South to Cambodia, Thailand, Malaya, Indonesia, Burma and the gates of India."[44] The same logic led President Kennedy to view Vietnam's poor land-locked neighbor of roughly 2 million as similarly important: "My fellow Americans, Laos is far away from America, but the world is small . . . its own safety runs with the safety of us all."[45] If the safety of the United States was tied to the fate of Laos, there had to be few places in the world to which it was not connected. In reality, communists did gain power in Laos and Cambodia after the U.S. withdrawal from Vietnam, and the humanitarian consequences in Cambodia were particularly horrific. But the falling dominoes, if it even makes sense to think in these terms, stopped there. Thailand, India, Japan, and Australia were not imperiled.

It was not only geographically proximate areas, however, that would be threated if the U.S. failed in South Vietnam. The repercussions were expected to be global. McGeorge Bundy, an advisor to presidents Kennedy and Johnson, explained that "around the globe, from Berlin to Thailand, are people whose well-being rests, in part, on the belief they can count on us if they are attacked. To leave Vietnam to its fate would shake the confidence of all these people in the value of American commitment." Dean Rusk, another adviser, expressed similar concerns: "the integrity of the U.S. commitment is the principal pillar of peace throughout the world. If that commitment becomes unreliable, the communists would draw conclusions that would lead to our ruin and almost certainly to a catastrophic war."[46] The rhetoric and predictions here are important.

44. Robert David Johnson, "The Origins of Dissent: Senate Liberals and Vietnam, 1959–1964," *Pacific Historical Review* (May 1996), p. 268.
45. Gelb, *The Irony of Vietnam*, p. 185.
46. Michael A. McCann, "A War Worth Fighting: How the United States Military Presence in Indochina from 1965 to 1975 Preserved Global Democratic Security," in Ross A. Fisher, John Norton Moore, and Robert F. Turner (eds.), *To Oppose and Foe: The Legacy of U.S. Intervention in Vietnam* (Durham, NC: Carolina Academic Press, 2006), p. 86.

If failure in Vietnam would have led to "ruin" and "catastrophic war," the costs incurred may well have been warranted.

In retrospect, Gaddis cannot "see how anyone could have viewed American credibility as being on the line in South Vietnam until officials of the Kennedy and Johnson administrations, through their failure to distinguish between vital and peripheral interests, unwisely put it there."[47] Gunter Lewy makes much the same point in slightly more sympathetic terms: "after three American presidents had declared that the independence of Vietnam represented a vital interest of the U.S., it could with much justice be said that the American commitment had in fact *created* a vital interest, for the prestige and credibility of a major world power cannot be dismissed as unimportant."[48] Of course, saying one's credibility is on the line does not necessarily make it so. Credibility depends on what others think, not on what you say or think. It is not at all clear that Soviet leaders doubted American resolve to defend Berlin, for example, merely because it was unwilling to keep fighting for Saigon, even if Bundy, Rusk, Kennedy, and Johnson thought they would. Lewy's observation also begs the question of whether the first of these three presidents was correct in characterizing Vietnam as a vital interest or whether repeated assertions to this effect made it so.

Differing assessments of interests did not drive all the debate over the war. Few, if any, antiwar protesters marched with signs reading "Vietnam is not a vital interest." But among those for whom considerations of national interest were paramount, there were dissenters rejecting the idea that Vietnam was even close to being a vital interest. One of the more ironic was George Kennan, often considered the "father of containment," the very doctrine so often used to justify the Vietnam War. Although he supported early U.S. efforts in Vietnam, Kennan eventually expressed deep reservations. In part, this reflected disgust with the military means employed. Imagery of fleets of American planes bombing a poor and less technologically advanced country at will repelled him. More important, he thought the effort being devoted to Vietnam was out of all proportion to its significance. Usually one to avoid the limelight, in 1965 Kennan became sufficiently concerned to testify before Congress

---

47. John Lewis Gaddis, "Were the Hawks Right about the Vietnam War?" *Atlantic Monthly* (April 2000), p. 132.
48. Gunter Lewy, *America in Vietnam: Illusion, Myth and Reality* (New York: Oxford University Press, 1978), p. 425, emphasis added.

continued

continued

and author a *Washington Post* editorial expressing his reservations about U.S. policy:

> Whatever justification this involvement might have had if Vietnam had been the only important problem, or even the outstanding problem, we faced in the world today, this not being the case, its present dimensions can only be said to represent a grievous disbalance in American policy. . . . the effects of this unbalanced concentration of resources and attention are unfortunate.[49]

In overreacting to the prospect of a communist Vietnam, the United States was like an "elephant frightened by a mouse."[50] Kennan's doubts continued to grow as U.S. involvement escalated. The following year, he could "think of nothing we need more, at this stage, than a readiness to relax, not to worry so much about these remote countries scattered across the southern crescent."[51] Although he continued to worry about the consequences of a precipitous withdrawal (which he would not call for until 1969), his basic view was clear: keeping South Vietnam noncommunist may have been desirable but it was by no means vital. It was worth paying *some* price, not any price. The resources and attention being devoted to Vietnam were just too great because "it is difficult to believe that any decisive developments of world circumstances would be determined in normal circumstances by what happens on that territory."[52]

Although Kennan gradually turned against the war, his fellow realist Hans Morgenthau was critical from the start. Like Kennan, he had no principled objection to U.S. military intervention abroad. "Intervene we must," he explained, but only "where our national interest requires it and where our power gives us a chance to succeed."[53] In the case of Vietnam, Morgenthau expressed doubts on both counts. In terms of interests, U.S. policy makers failed to distinguish between communist movements as extensions of the Soviet Union or China and those that were genuinely

---

49. George F. Kennan, "Is War Disbalancing Our Policy?," *The Washington Post* (December 12, 1965).
50. John Lewis Gaddis, *George F. Kennan: An American Life* (New York: Penguin Press, 2011), p. 592.
51. Walter F. Hixson, "Containment on the Perimeter: George F. Kennan and Vietnam," *Diplomatic History* (April 1988), p. 154.
52. Louis B. Zimmer, *The Vietnam War Debate: Hans J. Morgenthau and the Attempt to Halt the Drift into Disaster* (New York: Lexington, 2011), pp. 253–254.
53. Hans J. Morgenthau, "To Intervene or Not to Intervene," *Foreign Affairs* (April 1967), p. 436.

nationalist. Any victory for communists was mistakenly considered a victory for the Soviet Union or China. In fighting for South Vietnam, Kennedy, Johnson, and their advisors mistakenly thought they were "really containing the Communism of China." This "indiscriminate crusade against communism" obscured "the historic evidence of a millennium" demonstrating that "China is the hereditary enemy of Vietnam."[54] The Vietnamese communists were certainly willing to take aid from China in fighting the United States (and France before that), but they were not going to do China's bidding. Once in power they would pursue their "own national interests within the framework of communist ideology and institutions."[55] Kennan made much the same argument, predicting that "a Communist regime in South Vietnam would follow a fairly independent course."[56] Kennan and Morgenthau saw no reason to assume that a communist Vietnam would always side with China or clash with the United States. Zambernardi explains that, for Morgenthau, "only if communism had been an instrument of the imperialism of a foreign power, such as the Soviet Union or China, would it then have represented a threat for the national interest of the United States."[57] The national interest did not demand opposition to every manifestation of communism anywhere in the world. Unfortunately, "to cope with these different communisms on their own merit . . . requires an enormous subtlety of intelligence—which seems to be in short supply in Washington."[58]

Morgenthau also took issue with the credibility arguments. "Our very presence in Vietnam," he noted, "is in a sense dictated by considerations of public relations: we are afraid lest our prestige would suffer were we to retreat from an untenable position." He found this uncompelling, even perverse. In fact, he turned the logic on its head, wondering "whether we have gained prestige by being involved in a civil war on the mainland of Asia and being unable to win it." "Does not a great power gain prestige," he asked, "by mustering the wisdom and courage to liquidate a losing enterprise?" Although the question was rhetorical, his answer was obvious from the very manner in which he framed it. Morgenthau thought

---

54. Hans J. Morgenthau, "We Are Deluding Ourselves in Vietnam," *New York Times Magazine* (April 18, 1965).
55. Morgenthau, "To Intervene or Not to Intervene," p. 432.
56. Hixson, "Containment on the Perimeter: George F. Kennan and Vietnam," p. 156.
57. Lorenzo Zambernardi, "The Importance of Power: Morgenthau's Critique of American Intervention in Vietnam," *Review of International Studies* (2011), p. 1340.
58. Zimmer, *The Vietnam War Debate*, p. 80.

continued

continued

the United States was wasting valuable resources defending a nonvital interest, leading friends and enemies alike to question its good judgment, not its credibility.

Although Morgenthau's critique of the war was wide ranging, it ultimately boiled down to interests. "It is," he argued, "incumbent upon the government of the United States to define with all possible precision the extent of the American interest in South Vietnam. The extent of our military commitment must depend on that political determination."[59] He reached a different determination than most U.S. policy makers. Interestingly, many military leaders, like Morgenthau and Kennan, also "recognized the peril of intervention in Indochina" and "defined the national interest more narrowly than did the civilian establishment." Within the government, "the debate over Indochina policy" between civilians and the military was in large part "a duel over the nature of the national interest."[60] The same could be said for the debate in the nation as a whole.

Present: Syria

In the summer and fall of 2014, the actions of the Islamic State led the United States to conduct air strikes in Iraq and Syria, beginning what Americans were warned would be a long effort to defeat and destroy the organization. But this was not the first time the United States contemplated military action in the brutal and deadly Syrian conflict that began in 2011. The previous summer, before anyone heard of the Islamic state, many were already urging intervention on behalf of rebels trying to topple Syria's leader, Bashar al-Assad. Calls for military action reached a new peak in August and September 2013 with news that Assad's forces had crossed what President Obama deemed a "red line" by using chemical weapons against civilians.

The resulting debate encompassed several overlapping issues, including what type of intervention, if any, could be effective (e.g., no-fly zones, air strikes). The more basic question was whether U.S. interests in Syria were sufficient to merit involvement in a third Middle Eastern war in the span of a decade. Not surprisingly, there was little agreement. Despite opinion polls showing a war-weary public with little appetite for U.S. military intervention, President Obama argued that the regime's use of

---

59. Hans J. Morgenthau, "Vietnam—Another Korea?" *Commentary* (May 1962), p. 373.
60. Robert Buzzanco, *Masters of War: Military Dissent and Politics in the Vietnam Era* (New York: Cambridge University Press, 1997), p. 27.

chemical weapons and the conflict more generally involved the United States' "core national interests."[61] Not surprisingly, the national security adviser, Susan Rice, agreed, claiming that Syria's "use of chemical weapons threatens the national security of the United States."[62]

What were these core national interests? Precisely how was the security of the United States threatened? The administration and other advocates of intervention began with the obvious—Syria is located in a strategically important region and borders "our friends and our partners ... including Israel, Jordan, Turkey, Lebanon and Iraq." If the violence could be confined within Syria, there might not be much to worry about. But its impact was already being felt as refugees poured out of Syria and foreign fighters, some with terrorist ties, flowed in. Foreigners were willing, even anxious, to join the fight because they saw the Syrian conflict in terms of the larger religious–sectarian antagonisms dividing the region, not merely as a localized rebellion. Consequently, the conflict was likely to have consequences for its neighbors and the stability of a region long regarded as vital to the United States. Along these lines, Bill Keller of the *New York Times* favored intervention even before the use of chemical weapons because "we have a genuine, imperiled national interest, not just a fabricated one. A failed Syria creates another haven for terrorists, a danger to neighbors who are all American allies, and the threat of a metastasizing Sunni–Shiite sectarian war across a volatile and vital region."[63]

The Syrian regime's use of chemical weapons ratcheted up the pressure for intervention. Why? It was, no doubt, a particularly vivid reminder of Assad's brutality and determination to stay in power at any cost. But this was already evident. The issue was how and why the use of chemical weapons per se strengthened the case for U.S. intervention. Why did killing a thousand civilians with chemical weapons change anything when tens of thousands had already been killed with conventional weapons? No one, after all, thought the United States or even neighboring

61. Howard LaFranchi, "'Core' US Interests Now at Stake in Syria, Obama Says. Will He Take Action?" *Christian Science Monitor* (August 23, 2013). Accessed at http://www.csmonitor.com/USA/Foreign-Policy/2013/0823/Core-US-interests-now-at-stake-in-Syria-Obama-says.-Will-he-take-action/.
62. Susan Rice, "The United States Must Act in Syria," remarks to the New America Foundation, September 9, 2013. Transcript at http://www.pbs.org/newshour/rundown/rice-syrian-chemical-weapons-threaten-us-national-security/.
63. Bill Keller, "Syria Is Not Iraq," *New York Times* (May 5, 2013). Accessed at http://www.nytimes.com/2013/05/06/opinion/keller-syria-is-not-iraq.html?_r=2&/.

continued

continued

MAP 2.3 Syria and Immediate Neighbors.

countries were Assad's next targets. So why was the means by which he killed his opponents relevant? Some pointed to an increased risk of the weapons falling into the wrong hands. "Every time chemical weapons are moved, unloaded, and used on the battlefield," Rice argued, "it raises the likelihood that these weapons will fall into the hands of terrorists."[64] The more common argument, however, emphasized the U.S. interest in upholding legal and ethical norms against the use of chemical weapons.

"What message will we send," President Obama asked, "if a dictator can gas hundreds of children to death in plain sight and pay no price?" Inaction would make "a mockery of the global prohibition on the use of chemical

---

64. Interview with Susan Rice, *PBS Newshour*, September 9, 2013. Transcript at http://www .pbs.org/newshour/rundown/rice-syrian-chemical-weapons-threaten-us-national-security/.

weapons."[65] If Assad got away with gassing his own people, "other tyrants will have no reason to think twice about acquiring poison gas, and using them. Over time, our troops would again face the prospect of chemical warfare on the battlefield. And it could be easier for terrorist organizations to obtain these weapons, and to use them to attack civilians."[66] By this logic, *any* use of chemical weapons had the potential to threaten U.S. security in the long run because, as Rice explained, "*every* attack serves to unravel the long-established commitment of nations to renounce chemical weapons use."[67] Thus, the threat to U.S. security was not Assad or what he did (or would do) but what *other tyrants* might do *over time*.

The logic of this argument should be quite familiar. Here Syria becomes important by virtue of its place in an admittedly possible, but still hypothetical, chain of events. If Assad went unpunished, other tyrants would draw lessons encouraging them to take certain actions, the cumulative result of which could eventually harm Americans and U.S. interests, even if Assad's use of chemical weapons did not. In this formulation, Assad's use of chemical weapons threatens the United States only if it leads others to acquire and use them. Assad and Syria are not themselves threats to the United States.

There is also an element of domino logic in suggesting that any use of chemical weapons would set in motion a progressive erosion of a valuable norm whose preservation is a U.S. interest. In this case, however, the falling dominos are not nations succumbing to communism but inhibitions against using chemical weapons. Given the negative consequences of eroding this norm, it was best to shore it up when first challenged rather than to confront a tyrant or terrorist group that directly threatens the United States farther down the road.

The use of chemical weapons was also a turning point because the president indicated it should be. A year earlier, when he still opposed military intervention, President Obama was asked what might change his mind. He explicitly pointed to chemical weapons as a game changer: "we have been very clear to the Assad regime . . . that a red line for us is [if] we start seeing a whole bunch of chemical weapons

65. Barack Obama, "Statement on Syria in Rose Garden," August 31, 2013. Transcript at http://www.whitehouse.gov/the-press-office/2013/08/31/statement-president-syria/.
66. Barack Obama, "Statement to the Nation on Syria," September 10, 2013. Transcript at http://www.whitehouse.gov/the-press-office/2013/09/10/remarks-president-address-nation-syria/.
67. Interview with Susan Rice, *PBS Newshour,* September 9, 2013.

continued

continued

moving around or being utilized."[68] That red line having been crossed, concerns about U.S. credibility were inevitable. As Barry Pavel argued,

> Another, perhaps more important, issue at play is the credibility of the United States as an ally and security partner . . . Not only are potential adversaries such as Iran and North Korea watching, but competitors such as China and Russia and long-standing allies such as South Korea, Japan, Australia, and Turkey are watching too. If these nations perceive a lack of resolve . . . they might then be tempted to strengthen their own security in ways that are detrimental to U.S. interests.[69]

Thus, U.S. intervention was necessary for reasons that had little to do with Syria or Assad. The preservation of credibility was an interest in and of itself because its loss "might" lead enemies and allies to take actions "detrimental to U.S. interests."

Although many were persuaded by such logic, others thought it reflected a regrettably common "assumption that every nook and cranny of the globe is of great strategic significance and that there are threats to U.S. interests everywhere."[70] Far from involving any core interests or threatening U.S. security, the Syrian conflict was merely "another civil war in a country of little importance to vital U.S. interests."[71] Although willing to admit that the United States had vital interests in the larger region, Mearsheimer denied that the fate of Syria was among them. Although "the oil-producing states of the Persian Gulf are of marked strategic importance," "the United States has no vital interests at stake in Egypt or Syria" because they "have little economic or military power and hardly any oil." The United States should remain aloof from their internal conflicts because "what happens in those countries is of little importance for American security."[72]

Ironically, in a strict sense the advocates of intervention would probably have agreed. What happened *in* Syria did not really endanger

---

68. Barack Obama, "Remarks to the White House Press Corps," August 20, 2012. Accessed at http://www.whitehouse.gov/the-press-office/2012/08/20/remarks-president-white-house-press-corps/.
69. Barry Pavel, "What Was Obama Thinking?" *Foreign Policy* (May 1, 2013). Accessed at http://www.foreignpolicy.com/articles/2013/05/01/what_was_obama_thinking_syria_red_line/.
70. John Mearsheimer, "America Unhinged," *The National Interest* (January/February 2014), p. 9.
71. Jerome Slater, "Syria, Credibility and Armchair Isolationism," *Foreign Policy* (September 5, 2013). Accessed at http://www.foreignpolicy.com/posts/2013/09/05/syria_credibility_and_armchair_isolationism/.
72. John Mearsheimer, "America Unhinged," p. 9.

American security. Virtually all arguments for intervention, apart from those purely humanitarian in nature, emphasized what might happen *beyond* Syria—the conflict spreading to its neighbors, future uses of chemical weapons as the norm unravels, and rivals emboldened by U.S. inaction. There were counters to each of these scenarios. U.S. intervention could just as easily expand the conflict as contain it. The United States winked at Saddam Hussein's use of chemical weapons against Iran three decades earlier without the norm eroding. Other leaders would not doubt the United States' credibility simply because it avoided another Middle Eastern war. But the critical aspect of the case for intervention was not the specific arguments but the underlying logics by which the conflict in Syria was seen as threatening U.S. "core" interests and security.

The mere fact that all the national interest rationales had little to with any direct harm to Americans or U.S. interests is telling. Possible chains of events, an imperative to uphold norms, and concerns about the loss of credibility are what made Syria and Assad's use of chemical weapons significant enough to merit military intervention. For those inclined to a more restrictive view of core or vital U.S. interests, these kinds of arguments undermine the ability to differentiate vital from nonvital interests. This is what makes every "nook and cranny" of the world seem so important. The implications of such arguments made many uneasy. "With 'national interest' so capaciously understood," Eric Posner feared "the president will always be able to find a national interest justifying a military intervention."[73]

Thus, the debate over intervention in Syria in the summer of 2013 revealed a familiar tension. Those arguing that no core or vital interests were threatened viewed the Syrian conflict and Assad's use of chemical weapons almost in isolation. If Syria had little power, wealth, or oil, its fate was not critical to the United States. And if Assad was not attacking the United States or its allies, military intervention could not be justified. Others, however, connected the Syrian conflict and Assad's actions to something larger—a chain of events, a principle/norm, or U.S. credibility—revealing it as more important than it might seem at first glance. This is why some saw the conflict as threatening core U.S. interests, whereas others dismissed it as distant civil war of little consequence.

---

73. Eric Posner, "The United States Has No Legal Basis for Intervention in Syria," *Slate* (August 28, 2013). Accessed at http://www.slate.com/articles/news_and_politics/view_from_chicago/2013/08/the_u_s_has_no_legal_basis_for_its_action_in_syria_but_that_won_t_stop_us.html/.

CHAPTER 3

THREATS

Once the United States defines its interests and objectives, it must have some idea of what others want, what their interests and objectives are, because the outcomes it seeks will seldom be achievable by unilateral action or fiat. Whether the goal is containing hostile states, democratizing Iraq, opening markets to U.S. exports, halting the proliferation of nuclear weapons, or protecting human rights, other actors are usually in position to either help or thwart the United States. Achieving objectives entails influencing the behavior of these actors. Consequently, U.S. policy makers must know who supports and opposes their objectives and whose interests coincide and conflict with U.S. interests. No doubt it is useful to know what everyone wants—friends, adversaries, and everyone in between. Indeed, the initial distinction between "friends" and "enemies" is itself based on an initial judgment about intentions. Assessments of adversaries, however, are likely to be particularly critical and contentious because the consequences of being wrong are potentially so great.

The textbook case of a mistaken threat assessment that turned out badly is, of course, Germany in the 1930s. It is no doubt an understatement to observe that "if British decision makers had understood the scope of Nazi Germany's intentions for Europe during the 1930s. . . .

the twentieth century might have been much different."[1] U.S. decision makers did not fare any better than the British.[2] In retrospect, people often wonder how so many missed the clues about Hitler's designs and endorsed the ultimately disastrous policy of appeasement, a term that still resonates today as the ultimate insult in foreign policy debates in which being an appeaser is just about the worst thing possible. At the time, however, the situation was not so clear. A decent case could be made through the mid-1930s that despite Hitler's rhetoric and easily dismissed buffoonish bluster, Germany's foreign policy demands were limited and reasonable given the harsh terms imposed on it in the Treaty of Versailles that ended World War I. It was plausible to interpret German actions as legitimate revisions of a one-sided and unfair postwar settlement that could be accommodated within the existing order rather than a prelude to unlimited expansion and domination.

Those like Winston Churchill who saw Hitler's ambitions as more ominous and sinister thought acquiescence only emboldened him, encouraging future aggression. In hindsight, Churchill was right. Concessions did not satisfy Hitler; they merely whetted his appetite for more. But policy makers must make these judgments without the benefit of hindsight. What seems clear today was anything but at the time. The debate in the 1930s about German intentions is one of many illustrating both the difficulties inherent in threat assessment and the critical role perceptions of intentions play in shaping policy and fueling debates.

More recently, throughout the Cold War the United States and its NATO allies invested substantial money and manpower into deterring a Soviet invasion of Western Europe. The objective was to keep this critical region free of Soviet domination and firmly allied with the United States. This was the cornerstone of the strategy of containment. The policy assumed that the Soviet Union wanted to control all of Europe, not just the eastern states it occupied at the end of World War II, and was willing to contemplate the use of force if it could be successful at an acceptable cost. All the resources devoted to preventing this

1. Keren Yarhi-Milo, *Knowing the Adversary: Leaders, Intelligence, and Assessment of Intentions in International Relations* (Princeton, NJ: Princeton University Press, 2014), p. 1.

2. See Arnold Offner, *American Appeasement: United States Foreign Policy and Germany, 1933–38* (Boston: Harvard University Press, 1969).

invasion thus rested on *assumptions* about Soviet intentions and desires. They may have been reasonable, prudent, and even correct, but they were assumptions nonetheless. If they were right, all the effort and resources were wisely spent. If they were wrong, it was something of a waste. Either way, the Cold War policy of deterrence and containment, like the interwar policy of appeasement, was based on assessments of the adversary's intentions.

The basic dilemma and challenge policy makers always face is that "unlike the opponent's capabilities, which are directly discernable and thus frequently known with considerable reliability and exactitude, as a purely subjective phenomena intentions are not observable and thus not directly knowable."[3] During the Cold War, NATO could see Warsaw Pact forces stationed along the central European front, and spy planes, satellites, and other technical means of intelligence could look deep into Soviet territory. NATO had a good idea of what the Soviet Union *could* do. The problem was figuring out what it *wanted* to do. Policy makers will never be presented with photographs of Russian, Iraqi, Iranian, or North Korean intentions. Instead, they must divine or infer intentions from something they can observe. This is never a foolproof process. And because there is always an element of ambiguity and uncertainty in assessing something that cannot be observed directly, history is replete with faulty and intensely contested assessments of intentions. The inherent uncertainty about intentions creates substantial room for differing perceptions and, thus, debate about the policies that flow from them.

Inferring Intentions: Knowing the Unobservable

The dilemma of wanting or needing to know something that cannot be observed directly is by no means limited to foreign policy. In all aspects of life we rely on assumptions about how others are likely to behave. To take one mundane example, when you cross at a red light where cars are stopped you are assuming that the drivers intend to remain in place at least until you get to the other side. You are risking your life on this assessment of their intentions. But you can never know with absolute certainty what the drivers intend to do. Every one of them has the

---

3. Eric Nordlinger, *Isolationism Reconfigured: American Foreign Policy for a New Century* (Princeton, NJ: Princeton University Press, 1995), p. 99.

ability to speed through the intersection as you enter it. You cannot read their minds. You are making an assumption about intent and likely behavior based on things you have observed—that the drivers stopped at the red light in the first place as well as the behavior of countless drivers you have observed in the past. That you cannot observe intent directly does not obviate the need to make assessments as best you can. Nor does this uncertainty lead you to always assume the worse—for example, that the drivers will plow through the red light. It would be nearly impossible to go about our daily lives if we consistently assumed the worst about people whose intentions we cannot observe directly. Although it would be ideal if we could devise some means of observing intent, in reality we must rely on indirect, and thus imperfect, indicators. There is nothing new about this dilemma. Zachary Shore points out that "more than 2,000 years ago the Chinese military philosopher Sun Tzu urged his generals to know thy enemy. The question has always been how to do it."[4]

The options have not changed much since Sun Tzu's time. Broadly speaking, we can look to three things that can be observed as a basis for inference—what other states communicate about their intentions, the capabilities they pursue/possess, and their past behavior. That is, intentions may be reflected in (and thus gleaned from) what others say, what they have, and what they have done. Although each of these is somewhat problematic, they are used because there are no unproblematic indicators. Policy makers must rely on the evidence and information available to them, not on what they wish they could have.

What Others Say

Like U.S. policy makers, foreign leaders often talk about their foreign policy all the time, investing substantial effort into communicating and explaining their intentions and objectives to both domestic and international audiences. Through speeches, interviews, official policy statements, messages through private diplomatic channels, and summits where leaders speak directly with each other, there is usually a highly concerted attempt to convey and explain what they have done, what they are doing, and what they will do. In a few exceptionally rare

4. Zachary Shore, *A Sense of the Enemy: The High Stakes History of Reading Your Rival's Mind* (Oxford: Oxford University Press, 2014), p. 3.

cases, leaders have even laid out their vision in some detail long before they came to power, with Hitler's *Mein Kampf* being the prime example. This is perhaps the easiest place to begin looking for information about intentions, although the potential problems are easy to discern, especially for adversaries.

The most immediate difficulty is that these communications are not merely *about* a state's foreign policy but also a component of it. They are potentially strategic in being designed to help achieve, not necessarily reveal, a state's objectives. The purpose might not be to accurately convey what the state's intentions are, although there may well be times when it makes strategic sense to be honest. But anyone attempting to figure out another states' intentions must at least remain sensitive to the incentives for being less than forthcoming. There may even be reasons to be outright deceptive, to intentionally mislead and conceal intentions. During the 1930s, as some were raising concerns about German rearmament that violated the terms of the Treaty of Versailles, "German officials continued to reassure British decision makers in private conversations of Germany's peaceful intentions [and] its defensive motivation for militarization."[5] This should come as no surprise. States with hostile intentions rarely have any incentive to advertise them.

More counterintuitively, there may also be occasions when states might want to appear more hostile than they really are. Bellicose and alarming rhetoric can be a reflection of brinksmanship—that is, trying to convince opponents of one's resolve and willingness to bear costs to achieve a more favorable bargaining position. In this case rhetoric becomes an instrument of intimidation to secure concessions and may involve threats a state is not actually willing to carry out. States can bluff. This is a potentially dangerous game, but states may be willing to play it. Many have long wondered if this is what North Korea is up to. North Korean leaders and media may have elevated the art of bellicose and provocative rhetoric to new, almost comical, heights. North Korean broadcasts are almost surreal in their level of invective and nearly constant threats of war. The rhetoric is so over the top that the line between reality and *South Park* parody is almost nonexistent. But for many years this has been part of a fairly effective strategy for wringing concessions out of South Korea and the United States. Should North

---

5. Yahri-Milo, *Knowing the Adversary*, p. 67.

Korean threats be taken as indications of genuine intent? It is difficult to know.

A final complication is that hostile rhetoric apparently directed at other states may actually be intended for domestic audiences. Whether the goal is to divert attention from domestic problems to external enemies or to exploit popular sentiment to build political support, domestic and international politics can often intersect in complex ways that are difficult to disentangle. Leaders may view external enemies and conflicts as useful, and these political calculations could manifest in rhetoric that makes them appear much more hostile than they really are. When former Iranian president Mahmoud Ahmadinejad delivered fiery speeches threating Israel with nuclear annihilation, for example, did this reflect a genuine intent to start a war with a nuclear-armed state or was it the inflammatory rhetoric of a politician who knew what his audience wanted to hear, geopolitical red meat to arouse and inflame the masses? Or was it both? Unfortunately, "we cannot know if [Ahmadinejad's] observations were simply offered to produce a certain emotional effect, or whether they were evidence of intent."[6]

What Others Have

The assessment of threats requires judgments about both capabilities and intent. Hostile intent without the capability to do harm is futile, whereas capability without hostile intent is of no concern. If either the intent or the capability to harm is zero, the threat is zero. Because capabilities tend be more tangible, their assessment is considered the easier half of the threat equation. But even here there is uncertainty and plenty of room for error. On paper at least, the Iraqi military in 1990–1991 was large and formidable, the third or fourth largest in the world armed with all the sophisticated military hardware Iraq's oil wealth could buy. The tangible elements of Iraqi military power were impressive, leading many in the U.S. military to expect thousands of American casualties in 1991. But when the military intangibles of leadership, skill, and training were revealed on the battlefield, Iraqi capabilities looked different. Iraq turned out to be something of a paper tiger, demonstrating once again that military hardware does not equal

---

6. Posen, *Restraint*, p. 77.

military capability. Nonetheless, the general point remains valid: capabilities are *easier* to assess than intentions because they are generally more tangible. This offers one possible option for assessing intent: what if we could infer intent from capabilities? This seems plausible at first blush. After all, why would any nation pursue often expensive capabilities in the absence of any intent to use them? Thus, might it make sense to assume that nations acquire the capabilities they intend, or are at least willing, to use?

Although capabilities should probably be one element of assessing intent, there are reasons to avoid relying on them too heavily. To understand why, think about the United States. There is no doubt it has the military capability to attack almost any nation in the world. It was able to project force across the globe to depose Saddam in Iraq and oust the Taliban in Afghanistan. It has the capability to do the same in many other places. The United States' offensive military capabilities are awesome. Strictly in terms of capabilities, it "represents a standing threat to much of the rest of the world."[7] But surely it would not make sense for every regime that could be toppled by American military power to assume that this is what the United States intends. The United States has the ability to do many things it has no intent to do. If every nation that *could be* attacked by the United States acted as if it *would be*, the dynamics of world politics would be different and probably much more dangerous. Hence, it does not in fact make sense to assume that capability necessarily indicates intent, and nations do not appear to act as if it does.

A slightly more sophisticated version of this argument concedes that we cannot infer intentions from capabilities with any reliability. The ability to do harm does not necessarily indicate intent to do harm. The problem for policy makers is that "intentions are impossible to divine with 100 percent certainty . . . which means that states can never be sure that other states do not have offensive intentions to go along with their offensive capabilities."[8] What should policy makers do in the face of this uncertainty? Some argue "that because intentions are both difficult to discern with confidence and liable to change, cautious decision makers must always assume the worst about their adversary's in-

7. Robert Jervis, *Perception and Misperception in International Politics* (Princeton, NJ: Princeton University Press, 1976), p. 71.

8. Mearsheimer, *The Tragedy of Great Power Politics*, p. 31.

tentions and formulate policies on the basis of relative material indicators alone."[9] Although states with the ability may not intend to do harm, prudent policy makers will/should assume they do, playing it safe rather than risk being sorry.

There are obvious limits to this logic. France and Great Britain, for example, have nuclear weapons that could destroy all of the United States' major cities and kill tens of millions of Americans. They undoubtedly have the offensive capability to inflict substantial damage on the United States. But anyone who tried to convince the president of the need to prepare for a nuclear attack because we cannot be 100 percent certain of French and British intentions would likely be escorted out of the oval office in a straightjacket. Most Americans are comfortable assuming that France and Britain have no intent or desire to launch a nuclear attack on the United States despite their ability to do so. Even if it is impossible to be 100 percent assured that French and British intentions are benign, we can probably be 99.999 (and a whole lot more 9's) percent certain.

But France and Britain are easy cases because there is absolutely no reason to suspect any hostile intent. The problem is more difficult when dealing with states that have provided sufficient grounds to suspect at least some hostility. Making the worst-case assumption for France and Britain based solely on their capabilities would be ridiculous, but what about Hitler's Germany, Stalin's Soviet Union, Putin's Russia, Saddam's Iraq, Ahmajinedad's Iran, Kim Jung-Un's North Korea, or China? Although allies and obvious friends might be exempt, once a state is seen as a potential adversary, should worst-case logic based on capabilities kick in?

There are many variations on the advice that policy makers should deal with uncertainty about intentions by assuming and preparing for the worst. One of the more recent was the so-called "1 percent doctrine" attributed to Vice President Cheney in the immediate aftermath of 9/11 when the administration feared a wave of follow-on attacks, perhaps with WMD. In those chaotic days the administration, perhaps understandably, became sensitive to threats that might have appeared too unlikely to worry about just a few weeks before. In the wake of 9/11, Cheney thought the United States needed to reconsider how it responded to threats, arguing that "if there is a 1 percent chance that

---

9. Yahri-Milo, *Knowing the Adversary*, p. 7.

Pakistani scientists are helping al-Qaida build or develop a nuclear weapons, we have to treat it as a certainty, in terms of our response."[10] Because the consequences of al-Qaeda getting nuclear weapons were so potentially disastrous, even the smallest risk was unacceptable. Even if there was only a 1 percent likelihood that Pakistan intended to assist al-Qaeda in acquiring nuclear weapons, the United States needed to act as if it was 100 percent, an absolute certainty. The general principle is straightforward: if the potential consequences of a threat are serious enough, it should be treated as a certainty even if the chances of it materializing are slim.

The result of this logic could be seen in the Iraq war debate. The advocates for war feared that Saddam might provide WMD to terrorist groups that could use them against the United States or its allies. Opponents of war thought Saddam was extremely unlikely to share WMD. He had not done so in the past despite plenty of opportunities. Furthermore, he would probably be unwilling to place such dangerous weapons in the hands of anyone he could not control. As persuasive as these arguments might have been, no one could honestly claim that it was impossible, only extremely unlikely. As long as Saddam possessed WMD, the chances of him sharing them were not zero. For Cheney and anyone operating under a worst-case logic or the 1 percent doctrine, this was sufficient to warrant action. In the aftermath of 9/11, "Bush and his inner circle increasingly focused on what Saddam potentially *could* do with nuclear and other advanced weapons, and paid less attention to the probable *likelihood* of such actions."[11] Since the potential consequences of terrorist groups with WMD were so severe and the United States could not be absolutely certain Saddam would not provide them, it had to treat the possibility as a certainty.

Critics of worst-case thinking and the 1 percent doctrine worry that the consequences of applying this logic consistently would be disastrous. If the United States reacted to every extremely unlikely but potentially serious danger as if it were a certainty, it would be in a perpetual security crisis. If every terrible threat with a 1 percent chance of materializing were treated as a 100 percent certainty, the United States could be engaged in one war after another. And since the chances are

---

10. See Ron Suskind, *The One Percent Doctrine: Deep inside America's Pursuit of Its Enemies since 9/11* (New York: Simon & Schuster, 2007), p. 62.

11. Brands, *What Good Is Grand Strategy?*, p. 160.

low that the threats are real or will come to fruition, most of the time the United States would be overreacting, exacerbating conflicts and absorbing unnecessary costs.

In an ideal world, of course, intentions would be divined correctly all the time. In reality, the imperfect and incomplete information policy makers must rely on ensures that there will always be mistaken assessments in both directions, under- and overestimating threats. These mistakes in assessment can lead to errors in policy. If one assumes another state to be benign when it is actually hostile, the result is appeasement of the sort seen in the 1930s. If another state is perceived as hostile when it is really benign, the result can be an unnecessary conflict spiral, manufacturing a conflict where there was none. Worst-case thinking and 1 percent doctrines by their very nature are never going to underestimate threats. Consequently, they implicitly regard the dangers of overreaction as preferable to those of underreaction.

There are undoubtedly limits to what tangible capabilities can tell us about intangible intentions. The key debate is whether policy makers should resolve the uncertainty, particularly with respect to states already seen as adversaries, in favor of a maximalist estimation of hostile intentions. That is, should they assume and react as if an adversary intends to do the worst thing it is *able* to do? Or even in the case of adversaries, should policy makers rely on a more broad-based and nuanced assessment of what an adversary is *likely* to do? Is policy based on a worst-case reading of capabilities a prudent way of dealing with uncertainty or a recipe for unnecessary conflict? How policy makers and analysts deal with this uncertainty and the relationship between capabilities and intentions can itself drive a debate about policy. Agreement that Saddam was unlikely to share WMD with terrorists would not necessarily have led to consensus on how deal with him if some were willing to accept this small risk, whereas others insisted that even the smallest possibility be eliminated. Fortunately, one can also look to previous behavior to differentiate what an adversary can do from what it is likely to do.

What Others Do

On an interpersonal level, we generally infer intentions from behavior, not capabilities. We figure out what other people want and how they

are likely to behave in the future based on past behavior. People I encounter every day have the ability to do all sorts of terrible things to me
if they wanted to. They could beat me up out of the blue or attack me
with a knife. But since they have not assaulted or stabbed me in the
past, I assume they lack the intent and will not do so in the future. I am
not always right, but, thankfully, the vast majority of the time I am. In
any case, since I have not developed the ability to read minds or discov-
ered a foolproof indicator of intentions, my options are limited.

Similarly, policy makers can assess the intent of other states from
their behavior. That is, rather than relying on what other states *can do*,
focus on what they *have done*. This is among the reasons that no one
really worries about the French nuclear arsenal. Since the French could
have attacked any day since acquiring nuclear weapons in 1960 but
have not, we are probably on firm ground assuming they have no intent
and, thus, are not going incinerate the United States tomorrow. As
Nordlinger explains, "since a state's intentions are the most immediate
determinants of its actions, the latter serve as the evidence that reveals
them."[12]

As the absence of a French nuclear attack indicates, behavior includes not only actions but also inaction. If a state has consistently re-
frained from doing something it has the ability to do, this can reveal
important information about intent. The opportunities states pass up
can tell us as much as those they exploit. It is often difficult to recognize
and analyze nonevents because, well, they did not happen. But as
anyone who has read the famous Sherlock Holmes short story "Silver
Blaze" knows well, nonevents and inaction can be significant. In the
story, a Scotland Yard detective asks Holmes whether "there [is] any
point to which you would wish to draw my attention?" Holmes re-
sponds, "The curious incident of the dog in the night-time." The puz-
zled detective points out that "the dog did nothing in the night-time."
"That," Holmes explains, "was the curious incident." The lesson is that
a quiet dog may be just as important a clue as one that barks.

As with capabilities, using actions or behavior to infer intentions
can also be problematic. The major difficulty is that once we move
beyond simple descriptions of behavior to interpretation, it is not
always clear what behavior tells us about intentions. Soviet actions in
Eastern Europe in the years immediately after World War II are a case

---

12. Nordlinger, *Isolationism Reconfigured*, p. 102.

in point. There is little disagreement about what the Soviet Union did. Soviet forces remained in Poland, Hungary, Romania, and elsewhere after pushing Nazi forces back into Germany at the end of the war. After that, they imposed communist governments loyal to Moscow. Those are the facts. What these actions revealed about Soviet intentions, however, was a matter of dispute. In one interpretation, Soviet behavior reflected a profound, long-standing, and somewhat justified sense of vulnerability and insecurity only exacerbated by Germany's attack in 1941. Four years of war left much of the Soviet Union destroyed, with millions of military and civilian casualties, dwarfing U.S. losses of about 330,000. However undesirable Soviet actions were for the United States and the people of eastern Europe they were an effort to create a strategic buffer between the Soviet Union and Germany (and Western Europe more generally). In this view, Soviet actions were basically defensive. An alternative interpretation is that Soviet domination of Eastern Europe was merely the first step in a more ambitious plan to spread communism and Soviet influence, an early indicator of an inherently expansionist and dangerous adversary bent on controlling the entire Eurasian landmass and maybe even the world. These are not the only possible interpretations, but they illustrate that divining intentions from behavior is by no means an easy task.

A more recent example of the same problem was Saddam's attack on Iran in 1980. When war against Iraq was debated in 1990–1991 and again in 2002–2003, the Iran–Iraq war became a key piece of evidence in trying to assess the danger Saddam posed. Some saw Saddam's war against Iran as the first in a series of aggressive actions (he had just come to power in 1979), a risky gamble driven by his geopolitical ambitions and a glorified self-image. Others, however, viewed it as a calculated response to the threat posed by the new Islamic government in Teheran whose provocations left Saddam little choice. Although the war did not turn out as he hoped, Saddam's assault on Iran did not reflect any uncontrollable aggressive intent but rather a mixture of anxiety and opportunism in the face of a revolutionary regime seen as a threat throughout the region. As the debate surrounding the war in 2003 indicated, looking to an adversary's past actions seldom resolves the debate about intentions. The issue is not the actions themselves— for example, that Saddam launched a war against Iran in September 1980—but rather what motived and drove these actions.

These two cases illustrate the problem of using behavior to infer intentions—competing interpretations because the underlying intentions themselves are still unobservable. The purely descriptive details of actions do not say anything about intent until they are placed in some interpretation of why the action was taken. People believe their interpretations are so compelling as to be beyond challenge, but most of the time they are merely plausible. In reality, "actions are too often open to Janus-faced interpretations: the very same undisputed facts can all too easily be read as evidence of aggressive aims or defensive vulnerabilities; they lend themselves to about equally persuasive contradictory conclusions."[13] Consequently, previous behavior often becomes a locus of yet more debates about intentions rather than a source of evidence to resolve them.

The problem is not only that past behavior is susceptible to competing interpretations but also that there is often so much behavior to choose from. The Soviet Union, for example, had policies and took actions toward many countries that might have given contradictory indications about its intent. To say that we could learn about Soviet intentions by examining its past behavior opens a large field in which to search for clues. Should policy makers have focused on Soviet behavior toward Poland or Finland to infer its intentions? Similarly, what U.S. behavior and actions should others look at to infer American intentions? Not only is each piece of the behavior–intentions puzzle open to multiple interpretations, but also there are many pieces to examine. Because prior behavior offers so much to choose from "most of the time, the record is mixed—full of seemingly conflicting behavior, out of which opposing interpretations can easily be drawn. In other words, if one seeks evidence of malignant or benign intentions, both can usually be found."[14]

Another complication is that intentions can change over time. During the Cold War, for example, George Kennan viewed Stalin's death in 1953 followed by Khrushchev's rise to power as an opportunity to ease tensions with the Soviet Union. Since Khrushchev appeared to lack Stalin's suspicion, paranoia, and brutality (in fact, he eventually denounced Stalin's excesses), accommodation was possible with Khrushchev in power. This suggests that changes in leadership

13. Nordlinger, *Isolationism Reconfigured*, p. 102.
14. Shore, *Assessing the Enemy*, p. 5.

might alter a nation's intentions. What the Soviet Union did in 1947 might not have revealed much about what it intended to do in 1957.[15] A similar issue arose after Mikhail Gorbachev's rise to power in 1984. The question was whether he represented more of the same, with a friendlier face and more cheerful demeanor, or a genuine change. President Reagan thought Gorbachev was in fact quite different from his predecessors, an assessment that earned him some harsh criticism from conservatives who, although usually his supporters, thought he was being naive and seduced by superficial images and atmospherics.[16] But as would become evident when the Soviet Union's Warsaw Pact allies moved away from the Soviet model without any Moscow-led crackdown, Reagan was right. Soviets actions in Hungary in 1956 and Czechoslovakia in 1968, when it intervened militarily to crush reform efforts, were no longer good indicators of Soviet intentions in 1989.

Even without a change in leadership there is no reason to assume that intent is constant. We have already noted that Saddam's decision to attack Iraq in 1980 played a critical role in debates about invading Iraq in 2003. As we saw in a previous chapter, advocates of war thought the decision indicated Saddam's hostile and aggressive intent. Not everyone agreed. Either way, more than two decades had passed since his invasion of Iran. Much had happened in the interim, including his invasion of Kuwait in 1990, the subsequent war with the United States in 1991, and a decade of sanctions and international isolation. Perhaps Saddam, his objectives, and his intentions changed in the intervening almost quarter of a century. If so, his attack on Iran in 1980 may have revealed little or nothing about his intentions and objectives in 2003. Shore refers to this as the "continuity conundrum," the assumption "that past behavior [is] the best predictor of future behavior." Although this may often be the case, there is a danger of becoming too wedded to the proposition that prior behavior reveals the intent that will guide current and future behavior. One must remain open to the possibility "that new contexts could substantially change the enemy's intentions."[17]

---

15. See Hixson, *George Kennan: Cold War Iconoclast*, p. 139.

16. See James Graham Wilson, *The Triumph of Improvisation: Gorbachev's Adaptability, Reagan's Engagement and the End of the Cold War* (Ithaca, NY: Cornell University Press, 2014).

17. Shore, *A Sense of the Enemy*, p. 152.

Indeed, the possibility that intentions can change is sometimes offered as yet another reason to follow a worst-case logic based on capabilities. Even if we could be fairly certain that an adversary would not use certain capabilities today, the future offers no guarantees that a change of leadership or circumstances will not alter intent in a more hostile direction, perhaps quite quickly. Just because Saddam did not share WMD in the past was no guarantee for the future. Knowing an adversary's intentions today is difficult enough; knowing what they will be tomorrow, a year from now, or a few years down the road is truly impossible.

A final problem is that adversaries might not know what their intentions are—that is, there may be a disagreement within another state about what it wants. The language we use in talking about international politics often obscures this possibility. We personify states and refer to them as if they had brains and thought about things. In reality, however, states and governments are collections of people. It is people who think and have ideas about what their state's objectives ought to be. Realizing this, it is always possible that another states' intentions are a matter of contestation, with different policy makers, groups, or factions vying for control of its foreign policy. Thus, if we ask questions such as "will Iran abandon its pursuit of nuclear weapons?" or "what does China want?" there may be no clear, definitive answer. It is quite possible that "China" does not yet know what it "wants."

If an adversary's foreign policy goals are undetermined, in flux, and/or a matter of conflict, this suggests that policy makers face not only the challenge of determining their adversary's intentions but also the opportunity to influence them. Although there are many domestic and international factors that would ultimately determine the outcome of any struggle over foreign policy, one possibility is that U.S. policy could make a difference by reinforcing or undermining various factions. If there is one faction favoring a more moderate course of accommodation and compromise, some indication or signal that the United States would be a willing partner could help strengthen its position. If the United States rebuffs overtures and adopts a hardline position based on a view of the adversary as unrelentingly hostile, this could easily play into the hands of hardliners. The basic point is that competing factions may look to U.S. policy for evidence or confirmation that their outlook and approach is correct. To the extent that the United States can provide the necessary indications, it may help shape the adversary's intentions. When people talk in broad terms about encouraging moderates within other governments, this is the sort of interactive dynamic they envisage.

Conclusion

In his classic *Perception and Misperception in International Politics*, Robert Jervis observes that "differing perceptions of the other state's intentions often underlie policy debates. In the frequent cases when the participants do not realize that they differ on this crucial point, the dispute is apt to be both vituperative and unproductive."[18] There are at least two major take-away points here. The first is that disagreements about another state's intentions often translate into differences on policy. It is easy to understand why, particularly when it comes to potential adversaries, because perceived intentions are central for understanding the nature and magnitude of the threat and, thus, how one should respond. Such disagreements are evident even with administrations. During the Reagan administration, for example, "those decision makers who held more benign interpretations of Soviet intentions . . . often advocated more conciliatory policies and negotiations. Meanwhile, those who held hostile views of Soviet intentions . . . advocated more hardline policies and saw little benefit in negotiating with the Soviets."[19] Such differing perceptions are almost inevitable given the inability to observe intentions directly and the limitations of available indicators. There will always be some measure of uncertainty and ambiguity in assessing threats, and uncertainty and ambiguity are breeding grounds for disagreement and debate.

Jervis's second key observation is that people do not always realize the extent to which their policy disagreements are rooted in differing assessments of another state's intentions. This may be because people are often not explicit, either with themselves or with others, about their perceptions. Perceptions of an adversary's intentions are taken for granted and woven almost imperceptibly into arguments for policies as statements of fact rather than the potentially imperfect assessments they really are. This is unfortunate. Without being articulated explicitly,

---

18. Jervis, *Perception and Misperception in International Politics*, p. 58.

19. Yahri-Milo, *Knowing the Adversary*, p. 215. See also Keith L. Shimko, *Images and Arms Control: Perceptions of the Soviet Union in the Reagan Administration* (Ann Arbor: University of Michigan Press, 1991).

perceptions of intent escape the scrutiny they deserve, both in our own analyses and in the larger policy debates. This points to a need to be both explicit and critical, to always ask what assumptions are being made about another actor's intentions and on what basis they are being inferred. Although this will not allow us to overcome the problems inherent in trying to know something that cannot be observed or measured directly, we will at least be aware of how our assumptions influence the policies we favor as well as the possibility that they might be wrong.

ASSESSING THREATS, PAST AND PRESENT

Past: The Soviet Union and Détente

In the late 1960s and early 1970s, at the height of the Vietnam War and as the Soviet Union was approaching parity with the United States in strategic nuclear weapons, President Richard Nixon and his national security advisor (later secretary of state) Henry Kissinger tried to recast U.S.–Soviet relations with a strategy referred to as "détente" (a French term roughly translated as "relaxation of tensions"). Recognizing that the United States and Soviet Union would to continue to be rivals, détente nonetheless sought to place the competitive relationship on a more stable foundation. Given his strongly anticommunist background, it is somewhat ironic that Nixon attempted to ease the Cold War (as well as open relations with communist China). This was possible because "by the time he took office, the one-time ardent Cold Warrior viewed the Soviet Union as a 'normal' world power more intent on maintaining its position than upsetting the international status quo and therefore a nation that could be negotiated with."[20] This is key.

There were two main elements of détente. The first addressed the dangers of nuclear weapons by seeking arms control agreements based on a common interest in avoiding nuclear war and restraining the growth of nuclear arsenals. With thousands of nuclear weapons targeted on each superpower, there could be little doubt their use would result in mutual destruction. The concept of nuclear superiority was meaningless in this environment. Parity and sufficiency were the order of the day. Why continue the wasteful accumulation of strategically irrelevant weapons?

The second, perhaps more ambitious, element of détente aimed to modify the Soviet Union's behavior by tying things it wanted to changes in behavior the United States desired. If the Soviets needed "most favored nation" status to increase trade with the United States and access Western technology, the United States might expect less Soviet meddling in third world conflicts as a sort of quid pro quo. This "centerpiece" of détente rested on "the assumption that the Soviet Union could be brought, over time, to accept the constraints and responsibilities of a stable world order through that sophisticated combination of pressures

---

20. George C. Herring, *From Colony to Superpower: U.S. Foreign Relations since 1776* (New York: Oxford University Press, 2008), p. 771.

continued

and inducements known as 'linkage.'"[21] When linkage was combined with arms control, the overall goal was to "enmesh the Soviet Union in a web of relationships with the West, and above all the United States . . . to build a Soviet stake in maintaining cooperative relationships and in eschewing confrontations.[22] In Kissinger's vision, the Soviet Union was "both [an] adversary and collaborator," and détente was a strategy to "reconcile the reality of competition with the imperative of coexistence."[23]

The unresolved question, following Kissinger's framing, was whether the Soviet Union could really be a "collaborator" with whom genuine "coexistence" was possible. This answer depended, of course, on Soviet intentions and objectives. It takes two to collaborate. The expectation of collaboration and coexistence was based on a belief that the Soviet Union was a "normal" great power that sought these things as well. Those who rejected this view of the Soviet Union opposed détente, often vociferously. Thus, the debate about détente is best seen as a debate about the Soviet intentions.

If the United States and the Soviet Union were going to be adversaries as well as collaborators, presumably they would be the former when their interests clashed and the latter when they coincided. One area where collaboration was supposedly possible was halting the growth of nuclear arsenals, which by the early 1970s included thousands upon thousands of weapons with sufficient destructive power to wipe both superpowers off the face of the earth. The quantity of nuclear weapons, all many times more powerful than the bombs that leveled Hiroshima and Nagasaki, made nuclear war unwinnable in any meaningful sense. If a nuclear war was unwinnable with existing arsenals, more weapons would not make it any more winnable. Surely, then, there was a shared interest in bringing the arms race under control. Détente assumed that the Soviet Union agreed with the basic premise that nuclear war was unwinnable and, therefore, no advantage could be gained by building yet more warheads and missiles. How could anyone reasonably conclude otherwise?

Opponents of détente saw things differently. In their view, the Soviet Union did not accept the principle of mutual destruction. Right or wrong, Soviet leaders, who had seen their country suffer 20 million casualties

---

21. Gaddis, *Strategies of Containment*, p. 310.
22. Raymond Garthoff, *Détente and Confrontation: American–Soviet Relations from Nixon to Reagan* (Washington, D.C.: Brookings Institution, 1984), p. 30.
23. Henry Kissinger, *Diplomacy* (New York: Simon & Schuster, 1994), p. 742, and ibid., p. 30.

continued

during World War II and survive, actually believed that a nuclear war could indeed be fought and "won." "The strategic doctrine adopted by the USSR over the past two decades," Richard Pipes argued, "calls for a policy diametrically opposite that adopted in the United States by the predominant community of civilian strategists." Unlike American strategists, the Soviets emphasized "not deterrence but victory, not sufficiency in nuclear weapons but superiority, not retaliation but offensive action."[24] If true, this assessment of Soviet strategic beliefs suggested that even on this most basic element of détente—shared acceptance of mutual destruction in a world of massive superpower arsenals—there was a conflict between the United States and the Soviet Union. Consequently, opponents of détente saw arms control not as a collaborative endeavor to achieve compatible ends but rather as a contest in which the United States and Soviet Union operated at cross purposes. To make matters worse, the Soviets understood this and were more than willing to exploit American naivete.

For critics of détente, the naivete went much deeper than just a misperception of Soviet nuclear doctrine. This was only one manifestation of a larger problem. The entire logic of détente was faulty because it rested on an excessively sanguine assessment of the Soviet threat. Nixon was drawn to détente because he saw the Soviet Union as an essentially conservative, normal great power. Although there would no doubt be conflicts, the two countries could still do business, working together to achieve common interests while continuing to compete according to mutually accepted rules of the game. And even if the Soviet Union was not quite there yet, linkage could bring it along. The Cold War was, or could soon be, a fairly typical great power conflict in which coexistence was possible with the adversary and collaborator.

Although criticism emerged on both sides of the political spectrum, the most significant challenge came from the right as Ronald Reagan led the fight against détente within the Republican Party. Reagan's nearly successful bid for the 1976 Republican nomination against the incumbent Gerald Ford (who continued Nixon's policies and kept Kissinger on as secretary of state) was driven largely by his fierce opposition to détente. Reagan rejected détente because, unlike Nixon, he never wavered from his earlier staunch anticommunism. Although Reagan cataloged

---

24. Richard Pipes, "Why the Soviet Union Thinks It Can Fight and Win a Nuclear War," *Commentary* (July 1977), p. 33.

continued

what he considered the failures of détente (e.g., the continued growth of nuclear arsenals and Soviet meddling in Africa and Latin America), he also hammered home his more fundamental argument—détente could not work because the Soviet Union was not a normal great power. It remained what it had always been, an ideologically fanatical foe whose ultimate objective was global domination. The United States was not engaged in a typical great power rivalry involving both common and conflicting interests but rather in a life and death existential struggle against an enemy bent on destroying the United States.

Reagan's assessment of the Soviet Union would not change until Gorbachev's rise to power in the mid-1980s. In his first news conference as president in 1981, for example, Reagan pulled no punches. When asked what he thought Soviet intentions were, he responded, "I don't have to think of an answer as to what I think their intentions are; they have repeated it." He could think of "no leader of the Soviet Union since the revolution, and including the present leadership, that has not more than once repeated in the various Communist congresses they hold their determination that their goal must be the promotion of world revolution and a one-world Socialist or Communist state, whichever word you want to use."[25]

Many of his fellow Republicans as well as a sizable contingent of disaffected conservative Democrats rallied to Reagan's side. They joined him in opposing détente and urging a more hardline policy toward the Soviet Union, as did organizations such as the Committee on the Present Danger. Norman Podhoretz, a prominent member of the committee, assessed the threat the same way as Reagan: "The Soviet Union is not a nation like any other. It is a revolutionary state, exactly as Hitler's Germany was." It wanted not peaceful coexistence but rather the establishment of "a new international order in which it would be the dominant power and whose character would be determined by its national wishes and its ideological dictates."[26]

This really lays bare what drove the debate surrounding détente. If the United States was dealing with a normal great power, the idea that there   were   common   interests   on   which   agreements   and

---

25. President Reagan, press conference of January 29, 1981. Accessed at http://www.presidency. ucsb.edu/ws/?pid=44101/.
26. Norman Podhoretz, "The Present Danger," *Commentary* (March 1980), p. 39. See also his *The Present Danger* (New York: Simon & Schuster, 1980).

continued

accommodations could be reached was reasonable. The notion that a normal great power's behavior might be gradually changed in response to rewards and punishments is plausible. But if the adversary was out to destroy the United States, the very concept of common interests is difficult to accept. If the struggle was existential, it is easily cast as a zero-sum game in which anything advancing the interests of one side is necessarily harmful to the other. In this intellectual framework, any agreement the Soviet Union was willing to sign was automatically suspect. Anything the Soviets agreed to must be bad for the United States.

Since the critics of détente thought it was informed by a naive assessment of the Soviet threat, they considered it a one-way street in which Soviet interests were advanced to the detriment of the United States. Most obviously, Reagan and others pointed to the unabated growth of Soviet military power and increasing Soviet influence around the world. Détente and the optimistic assumptions on which it rested lulled Americans into a false sense of security, which in turn led to complacency and a shift of global military and political fortunes in favor of the Soviet Union. When Reagan finally succeeded in winning the presidency in 1980, he promised to reverse the damage he thought détente had wrought.

The goal of this discussion is not to judge these competing assessments of the Soviet Union or evaluate détente itself. The purpose is simply to illustrate how policies as well as the debates surrounding them can be rooted in differing threat assessments. Not surprisingly, it is Garthoff, the author of perhaps the definitive study of détente, who gets to the heart of the matter: "If international tension is seen as the product of perceived threats, détente can be characterized as the reduction of threat perceptions."[27] But détente was not merely an effort to reduce threats—it was based on a perception that the Soviet threat had already diminished from the scariest days of the Cold War. For Nixon, Kissinger, and others who saw détente as an opportunity to take some of the chill out the Cold War, a relaxation of tensions was possible because the Soviet Union had become a normal great power with limited objectives. Unfortunately for them, others still regarded the Soviet Union as an existential danger akin to Nazi Germany. And if the Soviet Union was a modern-day Nazi Germany, détente was the new appeasement.

---

27. Garthoff, *Détente and Confrontation*, p. 1083.

continued

Present: China's Peaceful Rise?

It should come as little surprise that China's meteoric economic rise over the past two decades has fueled increasing speculation about its political intentions and ambitions. Since threats stem from a combination of power and hostile intent, as long as China was limited in what it *could* do, there was little reason to worry much about it *wanted to* do. That has changed. China's growth has expanded its options, and its potential looking forward is tremendous. As a result, a veritable cottage industry assessing China's intentions has sprung up in recent years.[28] The basic question is familiar. In the 1930s people wondered what Germany wanted. Throughout the Cold War they debated what the Soviet Union wanted. Today, the $64,000 question is what China wants. There are two critical issues. First, what is the nature and extent of China's ambitions? And second, how, if at all, can U.S. policy influence what China wants as its power grows over the coming decades?

Much of the debate about China's ambitions is forward looking, anticipating what its foreign policy will be *if* its economic growth continues. At the moment, however, China's options remain limited. Despite being on the verge of becoming the world's largest economy, its military capabilities lag far behind those of the United States. Even on China's doorstep in East Asia the United States is dominant, and China lacks the ability to project conventional military power far beyond its shores. Speculation that China could one day become a genuine peer competitor of the United States is predicated on sustaining its current rates of growth for some time, which is by no means guaranteed. China is beset by a number of domestic economic, social, and political problems, any one of which could curtail its growth significantly. Although it is clear that China's

---

28. Henry Kissinger, the architect of détente, has weighed in on the subject with *On China* (New York: Penguin, 2011). For a small sampling of this vast literature, see Aaron L. Friedberg, *A Contest for Supremacy: China, America and the Struggle for Mastery in Asia* (New York: Norton, 2011); David Shambaugh, ed., *Tangled Titans: The United States and China* (New York: Rowman & Littlefield, 2012); David Shambaugh, *China Goes Global: The Partial Power* (New York: Oxford University Press, 2012); Nina Hachigian, ed., *Debating China: The U.S.–China Relationship in Ten Conversations* (New York: Oxford University Press, 2014); James Steinberg and Michael O'Hanlon, *Strategic Reassurance and Resolve: U.S.–China Relations in the Twenty-First Century* (Princeton, NJ: Princeton University Press, 2014); David Kang, *China Rising: Peace, Power and Order in East Asia* (New York: Columbia University Press, 2007); Robert D. Kaplan, *Asia's Cauldron: The South China Sea and the End of a Stable Pacific* (New York: Random House, 2014); and Christopher Coker, *The Improbable War: China, The United States and the Logic of Great Power Conflict* (New York: Oxford University Press, 2015).

continued

continued rise is not inevitable, substantial thought and debate have focused on what form it would take and how the United States should respond.

China's leaders have tried to assuage the fears of its neighbors and the United States. In a famous speech at Harvard University in 2003, Chinese premier Wen Jiabao laid out his vision of China's "peaceful rise." Not everyone has been reassured. John Mearsheimer is among those with a much more alarming assessment of Chinese intentions, seeing a future of intense conflict and competition. Indeed, he thinks the relationship will be so fraught with tension that a war with China is "more likely than was a Soviet–American war between 1945 and 1990." He concedes that this is neither imminent nor inevitable. A genuinely global challenge is decades away and may never materialize. The possibility is real enough, however, that the United States should assume that "China's rise will unlikely be tranquil" and prepare accordingly.[29]

Mearsheimer's assessment relies not on any analysis of China in particular but rather on a general assumption that the "ultimate goal of every great power is to maximize its share of world power and eventually dominate the system." In practical terms, this means that "the most powerful states seek to establish hegemony in their region of the world while also ensuring that no rival great power dominates another area." This is what the United States did. Mearsheimer expects China to do likewise. China will focus first on its immediate vicinity, undermining the United States' naval dominance while weakening its ties with allies (e.g., South Korea and Japan). The ultimate objective is "to dominate Asia the way the United States dominates the Western Hemisphere," which would eventually entail the withdrawal of U.S. forces. "Why would a powerful China," Mearsheimer asks, "accept U.S. military forces operating in its backyard? American policymakers object when other great powers send military forces into the Western Hemisphere, because they view those foreign forces as potential threats to American security. The same logic should apply to China."

Regional domination is only the beginning. China's ambitions will expand further if its power continues to grow. Like previous great powers, "a powerful China is sure to have security interests around the globe."

29. All quotes from Mearsheimer are from "Can China Rise Peacefully?," *The National Interest* (October 25, 2014). Accessed at http://nationalinterest.org/commentary/can-china-rise-peacefully-10204/.

continued

If the United States is not content to dominate only its hemisphere, why would China settle for just East Asia? If the United States has interests in the Persian Gulf, why wouldn't China? Mearsheimer sees no reason for China to accept less influence globally that its power would provide. Looking beyond East Asia, "China, like the United States, is almost certain to treat the Persian Gulf as a vital strategic interest, which means Beijing and Washington will eventually engage in serious security competition in that region." The United States cannot even expect China's activity to be confined to Asia and the Middle East. As the two become global rivals, "China will have good reason to interfere in the politics of the Americas so as to cause Washington trouble in its own backyard, thus making it more difficult for the U.S. military to move freely around the world." The Monroe Doctrine will not go unchallenged if China reaches its potential.

If this is what the United States can expect, how should it respond? The logic suggests the United States has an interest in stymying China's growth. Mearsheimer is blunt: "All of this tells us the United States has a profound interest in seeing Chinese economic growth slow considerably in the years ahead." Although this "might not be good for American prosperity . . . it would be good for American security, which is what matters most." He does not think there is much the United States can do to thwart Chinese economic growth. If it slows, it will be the result of internal factors over which the United States has little control. If it cannot prevent China's rise, the United States should prepare for it by implementing a policy of containment, much as it did with the Soviet Union during the Cold War: "American policymakers would seek to form a balancing coalition with as many of China's neighbors as possible. The ultimate aim would be to build an alliance structure along the lines of NATO." Outside of Asia, "the United States would also work to maintain its domination of the world's oceans, thus making it difficult for China to project power reliably into distant regions like the Persian Gulf and, especially, the Western Hemisphere." In short, the United States must ready itself for another Cold War.

For others, talk of containment, a new Cold War, and China challenging the Monroe Doctrine is wildly premature at best and perhaps dangerously misguided at worst. There is skepticism with regard to both Chinese capabilities and intentions. David Shambaugh, for example, argues that China is highly unlikely to continue on a trajectory that would put it in a position to rival the United States. Corruption, demographic imbalances,

continued

the absence of political freedom, a lack of technological innovation, and a host of other obstacles will keep China a regional power at most. "Scratch beneath the surface of the many impressive statistics," he urges, "and you discover pervasive weaknesses, important impediments and a soft foundation on which to become a global power. China may be a twenty-first-century paper tiger."[30] Zack Beauchamp agrees, arguing that "China faces too many internal problems and regional rivals to *ever* make a real play for global leadership."[31]

Even if China's growth continues, there are doubts as to whether it wants to challenge the United States' leadership role. On a regional level, at least, it seems clear that China wants to be the dominant player. According to *The Economist*, "what China wants in East Asia seems akin to the Monroe Doctrine: a decrease in the influence of external powers that would allow it untroubled regional dominance."[32] Toward this end, it has become more assertive in territorial disputes with its neighbors (e.g. Vietnam, the Philippines, and Japan) and is pursuing capabilities to undermine U.S. naval power in the East and South China seas. Although "the U.S. military has treated the western Pacific as its private pond," China has decided to "change the game" by increasing its naval power, particularly antiship weapons that would make U.S. aircraft carriers and other vessels vulnerable.[33] Although some believe the aggressiveness of China's regional moves has been exaggerated, most think it reasonable to assume, at the minimum, a desire to exert more influence locally.[34] The bigger question is whether Chinese ambitions extend much further. As we saw, Mearsehimer suspects that they do (or at least will). Others are unconvinced.

Seeing China as "a passive power, whose reflex is to shy away from challenges and hide when international crises erupt," Shambaugh senses little appetite for challenging the United States globally even if China was able to. Although recognizing China's assertiveness in East Asia and

30. David Shambaugh, "The Illusion of Chinese Power," *The National Interest* (July–August 2014), p. 40.
31. Zack Beauchamp, "China Has Not Replaced America—And Never Will," *The Week* (February 13, 2014), emphasis added. Accessed at http://theweek.com/article/index/256406/china-has-not-replaced-america-mdash-and-it-never-will/.
32. "What China Wants," *The Economist* (August 23, 2014), p. 47.
33. Mark Thompson, "In China's Sights: A New Missile Threatens the U.S. Navy's Biggest Warships—And Stability in the Pacific," *Time* (July 28, 2014), p. 34.
34. See Alastair Iain Johnston, "How New Is China's New Assertiveness?," *International Security* (Spring 2013), pp. 7–48.

continued

increasing ties and investments as far away as Africa, *The Economist* seems to agree: "for all its ambition, China is not bent on global domination. It has little interest in policies beyond Asia, except in as much as they provide it with raw material and markets."[35] Mandelbaum agrees that "Chinese economic policy is premised on the existence of the post-1945 international economic arrangements of which the United States has served as chief advocate and protector. China has as great interest in these arrangements as any other country. Economic considerations make China a champion of the status quo, not a challenger to it."[36]

The reference to China as a "champion of the status quo" hits on the critical point, answering the "the key question ... whether China has limited or unlimited goals."[37] John Ikenberry agrees with Mandelbaum that "China is not a revisionist power. It does not have big or contrarian ideas about the organization of world politics. . . . It will want more authority within the existing international order, and it will seek to alter the mix of rules and principles and institutions that constitute this order. But it will not be a purveyor of a successor order."[38] China is not the new Soviet Union. It expresses no missionary zeal to recreate the world in its image. More important, it is deeply entangled in the existing global economy. China's prosperity, which its leaders value so highly, is dependent on the order upheld by U.S. leadership. "It is true," Charles Glaser admits, "that China has disagreements with several of its neighbors." Nonetheless, "there is actually little reason to believe that it has or will develop grand territorial ambitions in its region or beyond." "The broader point," which often gets lost in discussions of its local squabbles, "is that although China's rise is creating some dangers, the shifting distribution of power is not rendering vital U.S. and Chinese interests incompatible."[39]

If this assessment of Chinese intentions is correct, the United States would be better off pursuing a policy of accommodation, not containment. As Betts argues, "accommodation would make sense if Beijing's ambitions were limited. . . . In accommodating Beijing, Washington would recognize

---

35. "What China Wants," p. 45.
36. Michael Mandelbaum, *The Frugal Superpower: America's Global Leadership in a Cash-Strapped Era* (New York: Public Affairs, 2010), p. 118.
37. Charles Glaser, "Will China's Rise Lead to War? Why Realism Does Not Mean Pessimism," *Foreign Affairs* (March/April 2011), p. 88.
38. G. John Ikenberry, "America's Challenge: The Rise of China and the Future of Liberal International Order," *The New American Foundation* (March 2011), p. 2.
39. Glaser, "Will China's Rise Lead to War? Why Realism Does Not Mean Pessimism," p. 88.

continued

that as China becomes a superpower, it will naturally feel entitled to the pre-rogatives of a superpower—most obviously, disproportionate influence in its home region."[40] What might this entail? Glaser suggests that "the United States should consider backing away from its commitment to Taiwan." In something of an understatement, he concedes that accommodation will "require some changes in U.S. foreign policy that Washington will find disagreeable."[41] In a similar vein, Robert Kaplan thinks the United States "must be prepared to allow, in some measure, for a rising Chinese navy to assume its rightful position, as the representative of the region's largest indigenous power."[42] Whatever the specifics, a policy of accommodation assumes that China can be accommodated and that its objectives are indeed limited.

There is one last wrinkle in the debate surrounding China's inten-tions: maybe China does not know what it wants. Elizabeth Economy admits the obvious in noting that "there is no real clarity as to what kind of global power China will become over the next critical decade . . . the international community is in the dark about China's 21st-century trajec-tory." This uncertainty results not only from the inherent difficulty of di-vining intentions but also "because there is no real consensus among the Chinese themselves."[43] There may be leaders and factions within China that want different things. Some may want China to displace the United States as the dominant global power and create a new international order in its image, whereas others may be happy to accept the basic fea-tures of an international order in which China has prospered as long as it is accepted as a great power with legitimate interests of its own. That is, the question of what China wants a decade or two down the road may be unsettled, a matter of political debate and contestation within China.

If this is so, some fear that policies based on an assumption of hostile intent might prove both self-defeating and self-fulfilling, creating the very threat it seeks to counter because "policies of containment and re-striction disempower those groups with the most to gain from warm

40. Richard Betts, "The Lost Logic of Deterrence: What the Strategy That Won the Cold War Can—And Can't—Do Now," *Foreign Affairs* (March/April 2013), p. 89.

41. Glaser, "Will China's Rise Lead to War? Why Realism Does Not Mean Pessimism," p. 86.

42. Quoted in "Troubles Waters: A Thoughtful Look at Asia's Dangerous Flashpoint," *The Economist* (March 14, 2014), p. 42

43. Elizabeth Economy, "The End of the Peaceful Rise? Even China's Elites Don't Know Where It's Headed," *Foreign Policy* (November 29, 2010). Accessed at http://www.economist.com/news/books-and-arts/21598956-thoughtful-look-asias-dangerous-flashpoint-troubled-waters www.foreignpolicy.com/articles/2010/11/29/the_end_of_the_peaceful_rise/.

continued

relations with the rest of the world, reinforce negative perceptions of the hostile intentions of others, and reduce the opportunity costs of a belligerent foreign policy."[44] An American policy of containment will be interpreted as aggressive, reinforcing China's worst fears that the United States will never recognize its interests and legitimacy. This, in turn, will play into the hands of those who want a more confrontational foreign policy. Following this logic, Jeffrey Legro recommends that

> when China espouses ideas and action that favor cooperative integration, it makes sense to do as much as possible to ensure that their internal supporters gain positive feedback and "I told you so" leverage vis-à-vis their domestic critics. Likewise, when China displays consistent revisionist tendencies, such ideas should be penalized— but *only* when influential groups are promoting more attractive alternative ideas.[45]

Thus, in the debate about China's intentions, the difficulty is not only determining what China wants and choosing the appropriate response, but also figuring out whether China even knows what its intentions are and crafting policies that might help shape what China wants.

---

44. Jonathan Kirshner, "The Tragedy of Offensive Realism: Classical Realism and the Rise of China," *European Journal of International Relations* (March 2012), p. 69.
45. Jeffrey Legro, "What China Will Want: The Future Intentions of a Rising Power," *Perspectives on Politics* (September 2007), p. 516.

CHAPTER 4

....

Tools

W e can think about foreign policy in terms of protecting and advancing national interests and objectives. Whether these interests/objectives are defined narrowly in terms of security and economic well-being or more broadly to include the promotion of values, their achievement usually depends on how other actors behave, not only on what the United States does. Consequently, foreign policy can also be viewed as an effort to influence international actors that can either contribute to or thwart U.S. objectives. This is another way of saying that foreign policy entails the exercise of power, which Robert Dahl famously defined as the ability of *A* to get *B* to do something *B* otherwise would not do.[1] U.S. policy makers in particular have many tools at their disposal for influencing the behavior of others. Choosing among them is the final piece of the foreign policy puzzle.

The potential instruments and tools of influence available to U.S. policy makers are varied and extensive. Partly for this reason, it is best to focus on the big picture, the major and enduring controversies about the utility of various forms of power in U.S. foreign policy. One way to frame these debates is in terms of Nye's discussion of "hard" and "soft" power in international politics. Noting that "power is the ability to alter

---

1. Robert A. Dahl, "The Concept of Power," *Behavioral Science* 2:3 (July 1957), pp. 202–203.

the behavior of others to get what you want," he identifies "basically three ways to do that: coercion (sticks), payments (carrots), and attraction (soft power)."[2] The first two—sticks and carrots—fall into the category of hard power, or the military and economic instruments used to induce or deter behavior through some combination of threats, punishments, and rewards. These are what people usually think of as tools of foreign policy—threatening or using military force, giving military aid, imposing economic sanctions, providing economic assistance, etc.

Although not denying that hard power is a necessary element of foreign policy, Nye lamented the tendency to equate hard power with power more generally, ignoring additional ways to get others to behave as one would like. He coined the term "soft power" to describe another, often overlooked, dimension of power. The difference is that "soft power is the ability to get what you want through attraction rather than coercion and payments."[3] With soft power, others behave as you wish, not out of fear of punishment or the promise of rewards but because they want the same things, making the use of hard power unnecessary. Whereas hard power is based on economic and military capabilities, a nation's "soft power can come from three resources: its culture (in places where it is attractive to others), its political values (when it lives up to them at home and abroad), and its foreign policies (when they are seen as legitimate and having moral authority)."[4]

Within this framework for thinking about power and influence in foreign policy, we can identify two enduring controversies and one more recent. Within the realm of hard power, questions about the use of force are always among the most contentious. The long-simmering debate that typically comes to a boil on the eve or in the aftermath of military action deals with when, where, and how the United States should use military force. The other recurring debate focuses on the utility of economic coercion and sanctions, perhaps the most commonly offered alternative to military force. The more recent debate, sparked in part by Nye's work and reactions to the U.S. war in Iraq, deals with the relative efficacy of hard and soft power in U.S. foreign

---

2. Joseph Nye, "Think Again: Soft Power," *Foreign Policy* (February 26, 2006). Accessed at http://www.foreignpolicy.com/articles/2006/02/22/think_again_soft_power/.

3. Joseph S. Nye, "Soft Power and American Foreign Policy," *Political Science Quarterly* (Summer 2004), p. 256

4. Nye, "Think Again: Soft Power."

policy, with many arguing that the United States relies excessively on its hard power, particularly military force, even when its use undermines American soft power.

Hard Power I: Military Force

Military power clearly looms large as an element of U.S. foreign policy. Globally, no other nation comes close to matching the United States in military spending and capabilities. In 2012, for example, U.S. military expenditures exceeded that of the next ten largest spenders combined (e.g., China, Russia, France, Great Britain, Germany, and five others).[5] The United States alone is able to project substantial military force to all corners of the globe. It has ten aircraft carrier groups, whereas the rest of the world combined has just one. The basic military realities have changed little since Paul Kennedy argued in 2002 that "nothing has ever existed like this disparity of power; nothing. I have returned to all of the comparative defense spending and military personnel statistics over the past 500 years . . . and no other nation comes close."[6]

The United States has also not hesitated to use its military power. Describing "modern America" as having an "unrivaled appetite for battle," *The Economist* points out that "during more than half the years since the end of the cold war it has been in combat. That is not just because of the war in Iraq, which lasted from 2003 to 2011, and that in Afghanistan. . . . Even before that, between 1989 and 2001 the United States intervened abroad on average once every 16 months—more frequently than in any period in its history."[7] This propensity to use military force may be unusually high of late, but it is by no means new. Looking back over more than a century, Robert Kagan sees the same pattern:

> Counting only the larger interventions, with "boots on the ground," there has been one intervention on average every 4 1/2 years since 1898. Overall, the United States has been engaged in combat somewhere in the world in 52 out of the past 116 years, or roughly 45 percent of the time. Since the end of the Cold War, the rate of U.S.

5. "The Uses of Force," *The Economist* (November 23, 2013). Accessed at http://www.economist.com/news/special-report/21590103-two-difficult-wars-offer-compelling-lessons-uses-force/.

6. Paul Kennedy, "The Greatest Superpower Ever," *New Perspectives Quarterly* (Spring 2002), p. 12.

7. "The Uses of Force," *The Economist*.

interventions has been higher, with an intervention roughly once every three years, and U.S. troops intervening or engaged in combat in 19 out of 25 years, or more than 75 percent of the time, since the fall of the Berlin Wall.[8]

Such figures suggest to some that American military dominance is a mixed blessing, offering policy makers a huge and ready hammer that encourages them to view every problem as a nail. But even among those who find this militarization excessive and misguided, few think military force can be avoided entirely; hence, the central debate over when, where, and how to use military force.

There is a familiar pattern to this debate that can be traced to the aftermath of the Korean War. The war's ambiguous outcome, with the Korean peninsula divided between the communist north and noncommunist south, was less than satisfactory. That more than 30,000 U.S. soldiers gave their lives for something less than complete victory was troubling for a nation that had recently fought Nazi Germany and the Japanese empire to total defeat simultaneously. Two schools of thought emerged in reaction. The so-called "never again" school thought limited wars like that in Korea should be avoided because, contrary to what leaders usually said, they did not involve vital national interests. In the rare event that genuinely vital interests necessitated military intervention, however, the United States should apply overwhelming force to ensure a quick victory. Alexander George characterized this as an "all or nothing approach" to the use of force, combining a general reluctance to intervene with a preference for massive force and decisive victory when necessary. The opposing "limited-war" school viewed such regional conflicts as regrettably unavoidable in an age of global superpower competition. The United States did not have the luxury of choosing how threats to its interests manifested themselves. Since the application of massive force would not always be practical or even effective, the United States needed to prepare its military to wage and win these wars, even if they were not the kind it preferred.[9]

8. Robert Kagan, "U.S. Needs a Discussion on When, Not Whether, to Use Force," *Washington Post* (July 15, 2014). Accessed at http://www.washingtonpost.com/opinions/robert-kagan-us-needs-a-discussion-on-when-not-whether-to-use-force/2014/07/15/f8bcf116-0b65-11e4-8341-b8072b1e7348_story.html/.

9. Alexander George, "The Role of Force in Diplomacy: Continuing Dilemmas for U.S. Foreign Policy," delivered at CSIS Security Strategy Symposium, Renaissance

Not surprisingly, a similar divergence was evident in the wake of Vietnam, a conflict whose outcome was even more unsatisfactory than that of Korea. The common refrain after Vietnam was an understandable "never again," although precisely what this meant varied.[10] As in the aftermath of Korea, some drew the lesson that military interventions in regional conflicts involving less-than-vital interests should be avoided entirely. Measures short of direct military involvement might be warranted, but the burden of any combat should be borne by local forces and allies. For others, never again meant that the gradual escalation of force seen in Vietnam should not be repeated. If the United States was going to intervene militarily, it should do so overwhelmingly and decisively from the outset. And reflecting the same sentiments as the post-Korea limited-war school, still others thought the United States had to be willing and able to fight the type of counterinsurgency war required in Vietnam because it was a harbinger of conflicts to come. The U.S. military might prefer conventional wars against national militaries, but this was not the reality it faced.

Although the United States is just beginning to grapple with the aftermath and lessons of its wars in Afghanistan and Iraq, the same arguments are already emerging. Although he did not like the direction of the debate as the United States began withdrawing from Iraq and Afghanistan in 2009, Michael Cohen was able to frame it in familiar terms:

> Unfortunately, the lesson seemingly being drawn from these two wars is not that the U.S. must avoid the sort of draining, manpower-intensive and time-consuming counterinsurgency operations that have defined the U.S. missions in Iraq and Afghanistan. Instead, the moral of Iraq and Afghanistan seems to be that the United States must learn to fight these types of conflicts more effectively, because they are the future of war.[11]

Washington, D.C., Hotel, June 25, 1998. Text can be found at http://www.pbs.org/ wgbh/pages/frontline/shows/military/force/article.html/. George also authored one of the classic works on the limited use of force, *The Limits of Coercive Diplomacy: Laos, Cuba and Vietnam* (New York: Little, Brown, 1971).

10. See Earl Ravenal, *Never Again: Learning from America's Foreign Policy Failures* (Philadelphia: Temple University Press, 1980).

11. Michael A. Cohen, "The Powell Doctrine's Enduring Relevance," *World Politics Review* (July 22, 2009). Accessed at http://www.worldpoliticsreview.com/ articles/4100/the-powell-doctrines-enduring-relevance/.

It is in these postwar debates that the enduring questions about when, where, and how to use military force are thrown into particularly sharp relief.

One of the more influential efforts to codify general guidelines for the use of force was articulated by President Reagan's secretary of defense, Caspar Weinberger, in 1984, slightly less than a decade after Vietnam. Weinberger's thoughts about the use of force, which journalists immediately dubbed the "Weinberger Doctrine," echoed the post-Korea never-again school and embodied widely shared beliefs within the U.S. military, an organization still reeling and recovering from the defeat in Vietnam.[12] Weinberger proposed six criteria, all of which he thought should be satisfied to commit U.S. troops:

> *First*, the United States should not commit forces to combat overseas unless the particular engagement or occasion is deemed vital to our national interest or that of our allies.
> *Second*, if we decide it is necessary to put combat troops into a given situation, we should do so wholeheartedly, and with the clear intention of winning.
> *Third*, if we do decide to commit forces to combat overseas, we should have clearly defined political and military objectives.
> *Fourth*, the relationship between our objectives and the forces we have committed—their size, composition and disposition—must be continually reassessed and adjusted if necessary.
> *Fifth*, before the U.S. commits combat forces abroad, there must be some reasonable assurance we will have the support of the American people and their elected representatives in Congress.
> *Finally*, the commitment of U.S. forces to combat should be a last resort.[13]

It is easy to see Weinberger's demanding conditions as a reaction to the Vietnam debacle. Although never adopted as official policy, "American military officials quickly put this doctrine to work in the mid-1980s to counter civilian demands that troops be sent into the maelstrom of

---

12. See Kenneth J. Campbell, "Once Burned, Twice Cautious: Explaining the Weinberger–Powell Doctrine," *Armed Forces and Society* 24:3 (Spring 1993), pp. 357–374.

13. Caspar Weinberger, "The Uses of Military Power," National Press Club, Washington, D.C., (November 28, 1984). Accessed at http://www.pbs.org/wgbh/pages/frontline/shows/military/force/weinberger.html/.

Central American revolutions."[14] This might come as a bit of a surprise to those who think the military tends to be gung-ho about the use of force, but this is one of those stereotypes with little basis in fact. Historically, the military has usually been more hesitant to use force than its civilian leaders.[15] The military likes to prepare for wars much more than it likes to fight them. The Weinberger Doctrine received Colin Powell's endorsement in 1992 while he was serving as chairman of the Joint Chiefs of Staff.[16] Consequently, this framework is also known as the Powell Doctrine or, to give both credit, the Weinberger–Powell Doctrine.

Many took issue with Weinberger's criteria, including his counterpart at the State Department, George Shultz. For some, any doctrine that reduced decisions about the use of force to a formulaic checklist was unwise, particularly if it essentially advertised U.S. reluctance to use force against potential adversaries. Others worried that Weinberger's conditions were so demanding they could never be met. An understandable caution in the aftermath of Vietnam had been transformed into a rigid doctrine of passivity. An understandable effort "to prohibit a repetition of the casual and ultimately disastrous intervention in Vietnam swung the pendulum to the opposite extreme of paralysis in the form of military inaction."[17]

Given the United States' recent experience in Iraq, a few critics of the Weinberger doctrine are reevaluating their original opposition. Frank Hoffman, still no fan, is among those at least having second thoughts: "Twenty years ago, I found the Powell Doctrine profoundly flawed as a codification of false lessons from Vietnam. . . . Now, in light of Iraq and Afghanistan, the benefits of this doctrine are far more

---

14. Walter LaFeber, "The Rise and Fall of Colin Powell and the Powell Doctrine," *Political Science Quarterly* 124:1 (Spring 2009), p. 73.

15. The classic work on this issue is Richard K. Betts, *Soldiers, Statesmen and Cold War Crises* (New York: Columbia University Press, 1991). A more recent study making the same point is Peter D. Feaver and Christopher Gelpi, *Choosing Your Battles: American Military-Civil Relations and the Use of Force* (Princeton, NJ: Princeton University Press, 2011), p. 25.

16. Colin Powell, "U.S. Forces: Challenges Ahead," *Foreign Affairs* 71:5 (Winter 1992/3), pp. 38–40.

17. Jeffrey Record, "Back to the Weinberger–Powell Doctrine?" *Strategic Studies Quarterly* (Fall 2007), p. 80.

apparent."[18] Michael Cohen is now fully on board: "the lack of attention today to the key attributes of the Powell Doctrine is difficult to
understand. After the twin conflicts of Iraq and Afghanistan, the more
than 5,000 American troops killed, the hundreds of billions—even
trillions—of dollars spent, it's hard to imagine a strategic doctrine that
is more appropriate."[19] The point here is neither to endorse nor to reject
the Weinberger–Powell Doctrine but rather to see it in much the same
light as the Commission on National Interests' analysis—an illustrative and thoughtful effort to wrestle with central dilemmas in U.S. foreign policy, namely those involving the appropriate role of military
force.

The most obvious of these dilemmas is evident in Weinberger's
first condition requiring vital interests before force is committed. Presenting this as a criterion begs the question of what these vital interests
are. To assert a necessity that vital interests be at stake raises as many
questions as it answers. For example, no doubt those who advocated
war against Iraq in 2003 thought vital interests were at stake, as did the
architects of the Vietnam War. As a guideline for when to use military
force, the Weinberger Doctrine or anything similar is not terribly
useful unless flesh is added to the bare-bones concept of vital national
interests, an issue we have already explored.

Even once this is done, however, we encounter another critical
question: should the use of force be restricted only to the defense of
vital interests? If we are talking about large-scale ground combat and
all-out war, one can understand why this might make sense. But the
"use of force" encompasses a wide range of options that fall well short
of this. Discussing the Syrian crisis, Barry Blechman, co-author of one
of the most comprehensive studies of "U.S. armed forces as political
instrument,"[20] highlighted just a few of the possibilities:

---

18. Frank Hoffman, "A Second Look at the Powell Doctrine" (February 20, 2014).
Accessed at http://warontherocks.com/2014/02/a-second-look-at-the-powell-doctrine/.

19. Cohen, "The Powell Doctrine's Enduring Relevance." It is somewhat ironic
that the author of the Powell Doctrine was secretary of state when the United States
launched a war that many think violated the doctrine. On this irony, see Walter
LaFeber, "The Rise and Fall of Colin Powell and the Powell Doctrine," *Political Science
Quarterly* 124:1 (2009), pp. 71–93.

20. Barry M. Blechman and Stephen S. Kaplan, *Force without War: U.S. Armed
Forces as a Political Instrument* (Washington, D.C.: Brookings Institution, 1978).

We've been overly cautious and unwilling to look at options between pure diplomacy and some kind of major military intervention. There are lots of things that could have been done early in the conflict, including demonstrative uses of force off the coast, while threatening to use air forces to curb Assad's barbaric use of air power against civilians. We could have backed that up by putting carriers into the Mediterranean in a highly visible way, or deploying ground-based air forces to neighboring states, and threatening to establish a no-fly zone if the Syrians did not stop bombing civilian targets.[21]

From this perspective, even if Syria was not vital to the United States, it might still have been important for a variety of lesser strategic or even humanitarian reasons. As we have already discussed, there are gradations of national interests. Blechman makes the complimentary point that there are similar gradations of military force.

Critics of Weinberger's approach argue that it obscures or ignores the possibility (perhaps even necessity) of calibrating the use of force to match interests. In Syria it may have made sense to take the options of "boots on the ground" and all-out war off the table. But should lower levels of force have been ruled out as well because the interests involved were less than vital? This is why Shultz and every other secretary of state has expressed reservations about the Weinberger Doctrine. As George explains, "Shultz observed that situations do arise when a 'discrete assertion of power' is needed to support our limited objectives. Shultz argued that diplomatic efforts not backed by credible threats of force and, when necessary, with use of limited force will prove ineffectual, resulting in substantial damage to U.S. interests."[22]

Those inclined to agree with Weinberger counter that once force is used, new dynamics are set in motion that facilitate escalation. What should be done, for example, if an initial limited use of force fails to achieve U.S. objectives? The logic of calibrating force with interests suggests that it might be necessary to walk away when the costs grow disproportionate to the stakes. At some point the United States might

---

21. "Barry Blechman on the Use of Force," *Cicero Magazine* (June 12, 2014). Accessed at http://ciceromagazine.com/interviews/barry-blechman-on-how-to-use-force-without-war/.

22. George, "The Role of Force in Diplomacy: Continuing Dilemmas for U.S. Foreign Policy."

need to cut its losses. But would U.S. policy makers have the discipline to do so? It is easy imagine why this could prove difficult.

The first problem is the "sunken costs." Even limited uses of force entail costs that represent an investment in a desirable outcome. If the United States walks away to cut its losses, the costs are essentially incurred for nothing. The investment yields no return. The dilemma for policy makers is magnified if the cost includes the loss of life. If the United States retreats rather than presses on, the sacrifices will have been in vain. This is a powerful emotional and political charge. And the greater the investment in an endeavor, the harder it is to abandon, creating an incentive to escalate further to justify the costs already incurred. After noting a sunken-cost theme in President Bush's case for redoubling U.S. efforts in Iraq as the situation deteriorated in 2005, Barry Schwartz returned to the obvious example to convey his discomfort: "As casualties mounted in Vietnam in the 1960s, it became more and more difficult to withdraw, because war supporters insisted that withdrawal would cheapen the lives of those who had already sacrificed. We 'owed' it to the dead and wounded to 'stay the course.' We could not let them 'die in vain.'" The logic was perverse in that "what staying the course produced was perhaps 250,000 *more* dead and wounded."[23]

The second obstacle to abandoning objectives as costs rise is the familiar problem of credibility. The logic is easy to surmise. The use of even limited military force signals a national commitment. If limited force fails and the United States opts to withdraw rather than escalate, the argument will invariably be made that this would be interpreted as weakness, leading potential adversaries to question U.S. credibility and challenge U.S. interests elsewhere. Some who opposed U.S. military intervention in Somalia in 1992–1993 as an unnecessary humanitarian mission involving no significant security interests, for example, worried that the Clinton administration's withdrawal after U.S. forces were killed in Mogadishu would damage U.S. credibility.[24] There may have

---

23. Barry Schwartz, "The Sunk Cost Fallacy," *Slate* (September 9, 2005). Accessed at http://www.slate.com/articles/news_and_politics/hey_wait_a_minute/2005/09/the _sunkcost_fallacy.html/. The 250,000 figure includes American and Vietnamese casualties.

24. See Charles Krauthammer, "The Cost of Promises," *Washington Post* (October 22, 1993), A23.

been no U.S. national interests in Somalia to warrant the initial intervention, but the intervention itself created an interest in the preservation of credibility. As a result, the danger is that an initial use of force creates a powerful incentive to prevail regardless of the less-than-vital interests initially involved because U.S. credibility is on the line and its preservation is vital.

To cite a more recent example, in the summer of 2014 the Obama administration initiated air strikes against the Islamic State in Iraq and Syria, offering a mix of humanitarian and strategic rationales. The resort to airpower has become a favorite form of limited force. Precision weapons and technological superiority allow the United States to take military action while keeping its soldiers largely out of harm's way. Assurances were offered that air strikes were not a prelude to boots on the ground or renewed combat for U.S. forces in Iraq, although "core" U.S. interests were involved. The logical question is what would the United States do if air strikes failed to achieve its humanitarian or strategic objectives? Is it reasonable to expect U.S. policy makers to simply accept failure after such a public commitment and description of the stakes? Thus, it is always useful think about and ask what the United States would do if limited force proves insufficient. Never assume or allow others to assume that things will go according to plan. The initial use of force cannot be taken back. The bell cannot be unrung. The use of force itself creates a new reality.

Those who favor a larger role for limited/discrete uses of force do not dismiss such concerns. The possibility that limited force might fail and set in motion an escalatory dynamic is real. It has happened. But in the overwhelming majority of cases, limited force did not lead to another Vietnam. James Jeffrey tried to calm some nerves regarding Obama's decision for air strikes against the Islamic State: "Do military actions of this sort open the door to a 'slippery slope' that could lead to new Iraqs and Vietnams? In theory, yes," he concedes. But he goes on to remind us that "the reality does not equal the fear. Over scores of deployments and combat operations since 1945, the United States has rarely headed down the slippery slope."[25] Furthermore, limited force can help achieve U.S. objectives. One study of 215 cases of coercive

25. James F. Jeffrey, "The PinPrick President," *Foreign Policy* (August 14, 2014). Accessed at http://www.foreignpolicy.com/articles/2014/08/15/iraq_obama_islamic_state_airstrikes_yazidi_maliki_abadi_war/.

diplomacy between 1946 and 1975 found that many were surprisingly effective, especially in terms of the United States' short-term objectives.[26] Another study reached the same conclusion looking at more recent uses of limited force from 1989 to 1996.[27] The lesson for critics of the Weinberger–Powell approach is clear: limited force often works and almost always remains limited. Vietnam is the exception, not the rule.

Future debates about the use of force are likely to continue to reflect these two orientations. They are useful frames for thinking about the use of force. Those generally sympathetic to the Weinberger–Powell approach will view force as an instrument to be used sparingly but overwhelming when vital interests are involved and less costly and risky alternatives have failed. Limited uses of force will be greeted with reflexive skepticism because their limited nature suggests that the interests at stake are not vital and they run the risk of further escalation as a result of dynamics unrelated to the underlying interests. Caution and a reluctance to use force are recommended.

This will contrast with the more traditional view of force as a critical element of diplomacy to be used flexibly in conjunction with other instruments of U.S. foreign policy. The ability to threaten and use force is critical for attaining U.S. objectives, and there is no reason policy makers should be denied this tool because the interests at stake are less than vital. As President Clinton's secretary of state Madeleine Albright argued, military force "doesn't have to be all or nothing. We should be able to use limited force in limited areas."[28] Parag Khanna is even more forceful on this point: "No self-respecting diplomat with a modicum of historical knowledge would ever pretend that diplomacy should unilaterally disarm and operate absent coercive threats."[29]

Hard Power II: Economic Coercion[30]

A perennial alternative to the use of force is economic coercion. Sanctions in particular have become a popular option for "doing

---

26. Blechman and Kaplan, *Force without War*.

27. Barry M. Blechman and Tamara Cofman Wittes, "The Threat and Use of Force in American Foreign Policy," *Political Science Quarterly* (Spring 1999), pp. 1–30.

28. Feaver and Gelpi, *Choosing Your Battles*, p. 25.

29. http://blogs.lse.ac.uk/ideas/2012/01/the-persistent-myths-of-soft-power/.

30. The classic work on the use of economic instruments in foreign policy is David Baldwin, *Economic Statecraft* (Princeton, NJ: Princeton University Press, 1985).

something" when there is little desire to use military force because they "occupy middle ground between political and military instruments in terms of impact, costs and risks."[31] When Iraq invaded Kuwait in 1990, the first impulse was to impose economic sanctions as the world debated whether military force should be used to liberate Kuwait. When Russia's actions toward the Ukraine took an alarming turn in the spring of 2014, the United States and its European allies imposed economic sanctions amid widespread recognition that there was no stomach for military action. Although economic sanctions have been used for centuries, their popularity has been on the rise of late:

> The end of the Cold War sparked a renaissance in the use of economic statecraft. The United States has been the most prominent and prolific actor to employ economic coercion . . . between 1992 and 1996 the United States imposed or threatened economic sanctions sixty times against thirty-five different countries. . . . [and] the United Nations Security Council implemented sanctions seven times in 1994 alone, as opposed to mandating sanctions only twice in its first forty-five years.[32]

The increasing resort to economic sanctions is not, however, the result of a consensus on their efficacy. In fact, most studies indicate only limited success at best.[33] Indeed, "the basic paradox at the heart of the sanctions debate is that policymakers continue to use sanctions with increasing frequency, while scholars continue to deny the utility of such tools of foreign policy."[34] There are certainly examples of both failure and apparent success. The United States has imposed a trade embargo on Cuba since Fidel Castro came to power more than half a

---

31. Diebel, *Foreign Affairs Strategy*, p. 244.

32. Daniel Drezner, *The Sanctions Paradox: Economic Statecraft in International Relations* (Cambridge, UK: Cambridge University Press, 1999), p. 7.

33. See, for example, Drezner, *The Sanctions Paradox*; Gary Hufbauer and Jeffrey Schott assisted by Kimberly Elliot, *Economic Sanctions Reconsidered: History and Current Policy* (Washington, D.C.: Institute for International Economics, 1983); and Robert Pape, "Why Sanctions Do Not Work," *International Security* 22:2 (Spring 1997), pp. 90–136. Pape is by far the least optimistic—whereas Hufbauer, Schott, and Elliot conclude that sanctions were successful in 40 of the 115 cases they examined, Pape's reexamination suggests the real success rate was just 5 of 115 (and several of those were on somewhat trivial issues).

34. David Baldwin, "The Sanctions Debate and the Logic of Choice," *International Security* 24:3 (Winter 1999/2000), p. 80.

century ago, which in and of itself is a good sign that it has not been terribly successful. On the other side, it is widely, although not universally, believed that sanctions against South Africa in the 1970s and 1980s played a role in undermining the apartheid regime of racial segregation and discrimination.[35] And more recently, many think that Iran entered into serious negotiations about its nuclear program in large part because of sanctions.

How are economic sanctions supposed to change an actor's behavior? With military force it is usually easy to understand how it is supposed to influence the target's actions. In the summer of 1990 the initial deployment of forces to Saudi Arabia was intended to deter further Iraqi aggression. The causal mechanism of this deterrent use of force is obvious—by increasing the potential difficulty and cost of an Iraqi attack on Saudi Arabia, deploying forces would reduce its likelihood. The following spring, the United States and allies altered Iraq's behavior by forcibly evicting it from Kuwait. But how would sanctions have worked to achieve the same objectives? What are the mechanisms by which sanctions are supposed to influence another state's actions?

The behavior of any actor reflects a combination of capability and desire, what it is *able* to do and what it *wants* to do. Economic sanctions have been used to alter both ability and desire. In the aftermath of Desert Storm in 1991, for example, trade restrictions were imposed on Iraq to prevent the importation of materials, equipment, and technology necessary to rebuild its military power and revive/expand its WMD programs. Sanctions beyond this were designed to impose pain and foment discontent with Saddam and his policies to induce his ouster or persuade him to abandon WMD in exchange for removing sanctions. Sanctions were supposed to affect both Iraq's ability and its intent to threaten its neighbors and build WMD. Similarly, the "primary goals" of sanctions on Iran are "making it more difficult for Iran to obtain materials for its nuclear program" and "affecting Tehran's calculation of the costs and benefits of continuing to pursue its nuclear

---

35. Even this is not universally regarded as success for sanctions. For a more skeptical view, see Anton David Lowenberg and Willian H. Kaempfer, *The Origin and Demise of South African Apartheid* (Ann Arbor: University of Michigan Press, 1998), especially Chapters 9 and 10.

program."[36] The reference to costs gets to the primary causal mechanism—sanctions are supposed to work primarily by imposing costs that exceed the value of the behavior you want the target to change.

Until recently, sanctions have been something of a blunt instrument, imposing economic pain on the target country as a whole in the hope that this would translate into pressure on governments to alter policies. The problem with so-called comprehensive sanctions (apart from the fact that they do not seem to work very often) is that "innocent" people suffer the most. Those in power responsible for policy often find ways to insulate themselves and allies. Comprehensive sanctions are indiscriminate, the economic analog of the mass aerial bombing of cities during World War II to induce the enemy to relent by making life for its people intolerable. To change the behavior of Nazi leaders, the allies killed tens of thousands of men, women, and children in cities across Germany. Although there is little evidence that this worked either, the underling causal logic was similar—pain for the people would lead policy makers to change course.[37] As Robert Pape explains, "economic sanctions seek to lower the aggregate economic welfare of a target state by reducing international trade in order to coerce the target government to change its political behavior." This can be done "either directly, by persuading the target government that the issues at stake are not worth the price, or indirectly, by inducing popular pressure for the government to concede."[38]

It is easy to see why comprehensive sanctions make many uneasy. Why, critics wonder, should children and other vulnerable groups in the target state who probably had nothing to do with what policy sanctions seek to change suffer the most? The cumulative humanitarian consequences of sanctions against Iraq in the 1990s were particularly worrying. Why should the people of Iraq, whose lives were already hard enough thanks to Saddam, have been punished further to get him to give up his WMD? The moral qualms embodied in such questions

---

36. Kenneth Katzman, *Achievements of and the Outlook for Sanctions on Iran* (Washington, D.C.: Congressional Research Service, 2014), p. 3.

37. The best work on strategic bombing is probably Tami Davis Biddle, *Rhetoric and Reality in Air Warfare: The Evolution of American and British Ideas about Strategic Bombing, 1914–1945* (Princeton, NJ: Princeton University Press, 2004).

38. Pape, "Why Sanctions Don't Work," p. 94.

create not only ethical dilemmas but also political difficulties in maintaining support for sanctions over the long haul.

Such concerns led some to wonder whether there was a way to impose sanctions while avoiding these humanitarian and political problems. Consequently, in recent years there has been a move toward a more finely tuned version of economic coercion commonly referred to as "smart" or "targeted" sanctions.[39] Unlike comprehensive sanctions, which are designed to "lower the *aggregate* economic welfare of a target state," with smart sanctions

> what matters is not the target's gross economic damage, but whether the target government and its key domestic constituencies feel significant economic pain from noncompliance. Smart sanctions are designed to raise the target regime's costs of noncompliance while avoiding the general suffering that comprehensive sanctions often create. Like precision-guided munitions, smart sanctions target responsible parties while minimizing collateral damage. Examples include asset freezes, travel bans, and arms embargoes, measures that stand in stark contrast to the comprehensive trade ban against Iraq.[40]

The underlying logic of comprehensive and smart sanctions is essentially the same—imposing economic pain to change the target's behavior. The difference is who suffers the most.

Largely because they are so new, "the jury is still out on whether [smart] sanctions actually work."[41] Their use against Russia beginning in the spring of 2014 is likely to become a test that will shape perceptions about their efficacy. In this case billionaires, banks, and corporations have been singled out for trade restrictions, asset freezes, and denial of travel visas. Richard Connolly explains the logic:

> The "surgical" nature of sanctions imposed so far suggests that Western governments do not intend to seriously harm Russia's economy or its people. Instead, the array of measures so far chosen—focused as they are on individuals and entities with close ties to

---

39. On the emergence of smart sanctions, see Daniel Drezner, "Sanctions Sometimes Smart: Targeted Sanctions in Theory and Practice," *International Studies Review* (2011), pp. 96–108.

40. Daniel Drezner, "How Smart Are Smart Sanctions?" p. 107.

41. Adam Taylor, "13 Times That Economic Sanctions Really Worked," *The Washington Post* (April 28, 2014). Accessed at http://www.washingtonpost.com/blogs/worldviews/wp/2014/04/28/13-times-that-economic-sanctions-really-worked/.

President Putin, his inner circle, and those with direct ties to the conflict in Ukraine—has likely been selected to inflict pain on key members of Russia's ruling elite, in the hope that this will force them to pressure Putin to change his foreign policy.[42]

Although there is no doubt that average Russians felt pain as a consequence of Putin's actions, this had more to do with the reaction of international financial markets as the Russian stock market tumbled and the ruble's value declined precipitously. This was an additional drag on an already struggling economy, in addition to sanctions.[43] The sanctions, however, were not designed to inflict generalized pain.

Given that sanctions, comprehensive or smart, are supposed to work by altering the cost/benefit calculations of the targeted state, the prospects for success depend both on the ability to impose pain and on the target's willingness to endure it. There are many factors affecting both sides of this equation. The more reliant the target is on international commerce, the greater its vulnerability. The more trading partners are willing to impose sanctions, the greater the pain. If sanctions are imposed by only one state or a small handful, the target may find it easy to escape their consequences by turning to alternative suppliers or markets. In contrast, the willingness to endure pain will depend on how important the issue at stake is for the target. Being pressured to change banking laws is one thing. Altering a fundamental feature of the state's political system is something else entirely. The costs imposed to achieve the latter will likely have to be much greater than to achieve the former. This is an important point because the pain of sanctions is a means to end, not an end in itself. Sanctions that fail to alter the target's behavior are just painful, not successful.

This importance of stakes helps explain the widespread skepticism that sanctions could induce Russia to withdraw from Crimea. Drezner was among those who did not hold out much hope:

---

42. Richard Connolly, "How Harsher Sanction Could Help Putin Turn Russia Back into the Soviet Union," *The Week* (July 25, 2014). Accessed at http://www.theweek.com/article/index/265328/how-harsher-sanctions-could-help-putin-turn-russia-back-into-the-soviet-union/.

43. Similarly, in the case of South Africa the issue was not only sanctions imposed by other states but also private movements to harm its economy by divestment. Formal sanctions were only part of the pain.

The current status quo for Russia is that they control that territory. In world politics, there is no greater demand to ask of a government than to make *de facto* or *de jure* territorial concessions. The domestic and international ramifications of such a concession are massive—especially after force was used to occupy the territory. So recognize that the demand being attached to the sanctions is so large that success is extremely unlikely.[44]

He thought sanctions could be more successful in other respects, particularly deterring further Russian moves against the Ukraine. Sanctions were more likely to persuade Russia to pass on something it did not possess than to give up what it already had. But even this depends on how much value the Russians (or Putin) attach to having greater control of Ukraine, something difficult to gauge at the time sanctions are imposed.

There are many other issues to think about in assessing the utility of economic sanctions. Do sanctions need to be tailored to the target's regime type (authoritarian or democratic)? Is the threat of sanctions as effective as their imposition? Is the target able to impose countersanctions (e.g., Russia cutting off gas and oil exports to European states)?[45] As with the use of military force, there are plenty of options, nuances, and details to take into account. But these should be understood within the basic logic of sanctions—altering the costs/benefit calculations of targeted states to influence their behavior. With this in mind, policy makers must judge what costs can be imposed and assess what costs the target is willing and able to absorb. Debates about whether sanctions can succeed will often be rooted in disagreements about how much pain can be inflicted and whether the pain will be sufficient to alter the target's behavior.

Soft Power

Thinking about soft power in foreign policy is complicated because it remains a "heroically imprecise concept, save only with respect to what it is not—hard power." Layne helps clarify matters some, explaining that

---

44. Daniel Drezner, "Bringing the Pain," *Foreign Policy* (March 7, 2014). Accessed at http://www.foreignpolicy.com/articles/2014/03/07/bringing_the_pain_sanctions_putin_crimea/.

45. See Risa Brooks, "Sanctions and Regime Type: What Works, and When?" *Security Studies* (Summer 2002), pp. 1–50, and Jon Hovi, Robert Huseby, and Detlef F. Sprinz, "When Do (Imposed) Economic Sanctions Work?," *World Politics* (July 2005), pp. 479–499.

when he first articulated the idea of soft power, Nye narrowed its scope and stressed repeatedly that soft power is about the influence of ideas and culture. . . . [but] as policymakers, foreign policy analysts and pundits . . . have come to use the term, soft power now encompasses a wide array of foreign policy instruments including: multilateral diplomacy, foreign aid, development assistance, the provision of international public goods, the exportation of democracy, national building.[46]

Thus, there are two main understandings of soft power. According to the first view of soft power, a "country may obtain the outcomes it wants in world politics because other countries—admiring its values, emulating its example, aspiring to its level of prosperity and openness— want to follow it."[47] The second view portrays soft power not as a generalized climate of support and admiration but as specific policy instruments that do not rely on economic or military coercion.

The first conceptualization of soft power is not new even if the label is. The proposition that the United States could be a force for good in the world by the virtue of its example as "a shining city on the hill" predates the republic itself as one of the earliest manifestations of American exceptionalism. Unlike leading figures in the French Revolution, the founding fathers saw no need to spread their political experiment by force of arms. Given its lack of hard power, the new nation was in no position to do so even if it wanted to. More important, it was unnecessary because the American system of government provided an inspirational model that others would surely want to emulate. The founding fathers can be seen as the nation's first soft power theorists.

Today this kind of American soft power is usually analyzed with reference to international opinion polls of attitudes toward the United States.[48] Negative trends in U.S. favorability following the invasion of Iraq were taken as evidence of an erosion of U.S. soft power. Nye worried that these "polls showed a dramatic decline in American soft

46. Christopher Layne, "The Unbearable Lightness of Soft Power," in Inderjeet Parmar and Michael Cox, eds., *Soft Power and U.S. Foreign Policy: Theoretical, Historical and Contemporary Approaches* (New York: Routledge, 2010), p. 58.

47. Joseph Nye, *Soft Power: The Means to Success in World Politics* (New York: Public Affairs, 2004), p. 28.

48. The two major global surveys that regularly ask these questions are Gallup (http://www.gallup.com/poll/142631/worldwide-leadership-approval.aspx/) and Pew (www.pewglobal.org/database/).

power in many parts of the world."[49] Poll after poll indicated that the decision for war without United Nations sanction, the failure to find WMD in Iraq, the indefinite detention of prisoners at Guantanamo, and reports of torture took a toll on the United States' standing in much of the world.

Why is this important? International politics, after all, is not a popularity contest. In some senses, soft power advocates argue it is. The underlying assumption is that if the United States and its policies are viewed favorably, other nations will be more inclined to support it. Admiration for the United States and a belief that it respects the views, wishes, and interests of others creates an environment conducive to achieving its objectives. Nye warns that "when we discount the importance of our attractiveness to other countries we pay a price . . . if the United States is so unpopular in a country that being pro-American is the kiss of death in their domestic politics, political leaders are unlikely to make concessions to help us."[50] A reservoir of goodwill makes life a lot easier for U.S. policy makers than a well of anger, suspicion, and resentment.

At this level soft power theorists urge policy makers to remain cognizant of how American policies can undermine or enhance its legitimacy and global leadership. Positive perceptions make it easier for the United States to get the cooperation and support it often needs. The argument is not that the United States should always refrain from doing anything unpopular. There may indeed be situations in which the United States must take actions that meet with international disapproval. Other nations should not have a veto on U.S. foreign policy. The point is simply to recognize the benefits of being viewed favorably as well as the costs of alienating those whose cooperation and help might be important. Maintaining soft power is a matter of self-interest, not deference.

The policy instrument view of soft power was recently reflected in David Rhode's recent effort to "reimagine American influence in the

---

49. "Interview: Dr. Joseph Nye, Jr.," *Diplomatic Courier* (June 21, 2012). Accessed athttp://www.diplomaticourier.com/news/topics/diplomacy/1368-interview-dr-joseph-nye-jr/.

50. Nye, "Soft Power and American Foreign Policy," p. 257. See also Joseph Nye, "The Decline of America's Soft Power: Why Washington Should Worry," *Foreign Affairs* (May–June 2004), pp. 16–20.

Middle East." In criticizing the United States' reliance on military force to achieve its objectives, he relates how in the aftermath of the Arab Spring in 2011 the United States sent a delegation of private-sector representatives from technology industries to advise entrepreneurs trying to launch new ventures in Tunisia. This is precisely the sort of endeavor the United States always claimed it wanted to encourage—political *and* economic reform as a long-term solution to the political repression and economic frustration that fueled instability and violence in the region. Advice and knowledge of this sort can help achieve the outcomes the United States wants but cannot be thought of as either a reward or a punishment, a carrot or a stick. But when it came time for the delegation to make the journey, its members had to buy their own tickets.[51] The penny-pinching absurdity here is mind-boggling and telling. A nation willing to spend hundreds of billions of dollars waging two wars to bring political change in the region was unwilling (it was certainly able) to purchase a few economy-class tickets for a few thousand dollars to promote economic growth and development. For advocates of soft power, this speaks volumes about the neglect of the nonmilitary tools of U.S. foreign policy, leading Rhode to argue that "American policymakers must change their antiquated concept of national power" if they want to promote economic development, political democracy, and ideological moderation in the Middle East.[52]

Rhode has some surprisingly allies. Former secretary of defense Robert Gates agreed, often finding himself in the odd position of pleading for more State Department funding. Although recognizing that "funding for non-military foreign affairs programs has increased," it nonetheless "remains disproportionately small relative to what we spend on the military and to the importance of such capabilities." Gates pointed to the somewhat startling fact that the State Department's entire budget is less than what the Pentagon spends on health care alone.

Echoing the sentiments of Nye and Rhode, Gates frequently lamented the lack of support for "America's ability to engage, assist, and communicate with other parts of the world—the 'soft power,' which

51. David Rhode, *Beyond War: Reimagining American Influence in the Middle East* (New York: Viking, 2013), p. 108.
52. Ibid., p. 169.

had been so important throughout the Cold War."[53] Not surprisingly, he highlighted the U.S. experience in Iraq. In terms of U.S. hard power, there was little doubt about its effectiveness for ousting Saddam. But this was not the ultimate objective. The United States was also concerned with the nature of the regime that replaced him. The preference was for a stable, hopefully somewhat democratic and economically prosperous Iraq that no longer pursued WMD or threatened its neighbors. The necessary political, economic, judicial, and law-enforcement institutions, however, were not just going to appear on their own after decades of brutality, misrule, and corruption, and U.S. military forces were neither trained nor equipped to create them.

Once Saddam and the Baathist regime was out of the way, the United States found that its capacity to provide the resources, expertise, and advisors to build these vital institutions was limited. The juxtaposition of these different types of power in Iraq was striking: there were tens of thousands of well-trained soldiers and billions of dollars available to get rid of Saddam's regime by force but no comparable battalions of equally well-funded civilians trained to do everything necessary to create the sort of country the United States wanted in its place.

Interestingly, it is virtually impossible to find anyone inside or outside the military who disagrees. At least in the abstract there is widespread agreement about the need for investment in both military and nonmilitary capabilities, hard and soft power, to use alone or in combination In reality, however, the mere fact that the secretary of defense, of all people, must lobby Congress for nonmilitary programs suggests that the advocates of soft power face an uphill battle getting a larger share of foreign policy resources.

Why the chronic disparity between the tremendous resources devoted to military hard power and the pittance allocated to soft power? No doubt there is some element of politics at play—defense spending has powerful interests and constituencies that drive expenditures and protect it from the budgetary ax. But part of the answer may also lie in the nature of soft power itself. One of the benefits of hard, particularly military, power is its immediacy. When Iraqis (with some American help) toppled the huge statue of Saddam in Baghdad's Firdos Square after U.S. forces captured the city, the evening news provided a

---

53. Robert Gates, "The Landon Lecture at Kansas State University," November 26, 2007. Accessed at http://www.defense.gov/speeches/speech.aspx?speechid=1199/.

particularly vivid image of American hard power at work. The connection between soft power and outcomes is almost never this obvious.
The successes of aid programs, educational and cultural exchanges,
and communication strategies are measured gradually over months
and years in small but important increments. The investment in soft
power seldom yields immediate and dramatic returns. The use of soft
power to achieve foreign objectives requires a decent degree of delayed
gratification. With hard power, the bang you get for your buck is louder.
There is a reason it is referred to as "soft" power.

This might be why there has been an effort recently to rebrand soft
power so that it does not appear so, well, soft. Nye and others explain
that they never viewed soft power as a replacement for hard power.
They complained about the inordinate emphasis on, and investment in,
hard power compared to soft. It was a matter of striking the appropriate balance between the two. Like Gates, Nye pointed to the United
States' triumph in the Cold War: "During the Cold War, the West used
hard power to deter Soviet aggression, while it also used soft power to
erode faith in Communism behind the iron curtain." As American and
allied forces kept the Soviet Union at bay through containment and
deterrence, knowledge of Western democracy, human rights, and prosperity ate away at the fabric of the Soviet system, denying it the legitimacy and appeal any system needs to survive in the long term.
Consequently, it is better to think not in terms of hard or soft power but
in a combination of the two, an amalgam now routinely referred to as
"smart power," or "the ability to combine the hard power of coercion or
payment with the soft power of attraction into a successful strategy."[54]
Former Secretary of State Clinton adopted this new terminology, arguing that "we must use what has been called smart power, the full range
of tools at our disposal—diplomatic, economic, military, political,
legal, and cultural—picking the right tool or combination of tools for
each situation."[55] That the term smart power appeared in the wake of
the September 11 attacks, when few Americans were in the mood to be

----

54. Nye, "Think Again: Soft Power." It is not clear who coined the term smart
power. Most think it was Nye, but there is a case for it being Suzanne Nossel (see her
"Smart Power: Reclaiming Liberal Internationalism," *Foreign Affairs* (March–April
2004).

55. Eric Etheridge, "How 'Soft' Power Got 'Smart,'" *New York Times* (January 14,
2009). Accessed at http://opinionator.blogs.nytimes.com/2009/01/14/how-soft-power-
got-smart/.

soft about anything, is surely no coincidence. If the choice was between soft and hard power, the latter was likely to be preferred. But if the choice is between smart power and its alternative (stupid power?), the decision is a no-brainer.

Conclusion

There is one final challenge in thinking about American foreign policy and power. Amid persistent calls for U.S. intervention in the Middle East in the summer of 2014 to deal with the conflict in Syria and the associated rise and spread of the Islamic State, Kevin Drum thought the dilemma confronting U.S. policy makers was even more fundamental than many realized. It was not a matter of selecting the right policy instruments. In Drum's view, the real problem was that none of the feasible options would achieve U.S. objectives:

> It's human nature to believe that intervention is always better than doing nothing. Liberals tend to believe this in domestic affairs and conservatives tend to believe it in foreign affairs. But it's not always so. The Middle East suffers from fundamental, longstanding fractures that the United States simply can't affect other than at the margins. Think about it this way: What are the odds that shipping arms and supplies to a poorly defined, poorly coordinated, and poorly understood rebel alliance in Syria would make a significant difference in the long-term outcome there when two decade-long wars in Afghanistan and Iraq barely changed anything?[56]

Regardless of whether Drum was right in this particular case, the general proposition that policy makers may encounter problems American power cannot solve or desired outcomes that cannot be achieved must be entertained.

This suggests a need to think not only about *what* the United States wants to accomplish and *how* to accomplish it, but also about *whether* it can achieve what it desires. One is reminded of the so-called serenity prayer familiar to even many nonreligious people: "God, grant me the serenity to accept the things I cannot change, the courage to change the things I can, and the wisdom to know the difference." Attributed to

---

56. Kevin Drum, "Arming the Syrian Rebels Wouldn't Have Stopped Isis," *Mother Jones* (August 13, 2014). Accessed at http://www.motherjones.com/kevin-drum/2014/08/syria/.

the American theologian Reinhold Neibuhr, the prayer combines a laudable measure of ambition with humility, idealism tempered by re-alism. Although today it is more likely to be recited in various twelve-step recovery programs than in the State or Defense departments, the serenity prayer contains more than a little insight for those thinking about the utility of various forms of American power. The last (or maybe first) critical question is not which instruments will be effective, but whether any of them will be. Even a nation as powerful as the United States must recognize, confront, and identify not merely the complicated choices involved in its use of power but also the limits of its power, hard, soft, or smart. Power is not only multidimensional; it is also finite.[57]

---

57. I borrowed this terminology from Brands, *What Good Is Grand Strategy?*, p. 204.

EVALUATING TOOLS, PAST AND PRESENT

Past: Iraq and Economic Sanctions, 1990–1991

Iraq's invasion, conquest, and brutal occupation of Kuwait in early August 1990 was greeted with as close to universal condemnation as one is ever likely to encounter in international politics. Few events have so united and galvanized the international community before or since. No one wanted to legitimize Saddam's annexation of Kuwait by recognizing it as Iraq's newest province. The first order of business that August, however, was deterring an Iraqi move on Saudi Arabia. Once the Saudis accepted U.S. forces on their territory, off they went with little dissent or debate in the United States. With that out of the way, the trickier dilemma remained. If Saddam was to be denied the fruits of his aggression, his forces would ultimately have to leave Kuwait. But why would Saddam remove them? What would induce him to give up what he had just acquired and now controlled? A chorus of international disapproval and criticism, which he no doubt expected, was unlikely to convince him to leave. There seemed to be two options—economic or military coercion. This is where unity, both within the United States and internationally, broke down. There was agreement on the goal of Iraq leaving and Kuwaiti independence being restored. On the means to this end there was no consensus.

There were good reasons not to rush to military action. The prospect of unleashing a war in one of the world's most volatile regions was not something anyone looked forward to. There was no telling what Saddam, armed with chemical weapons, might do to avoid defeat. And in the United States, especially within its military, the ghost of Vietnam was ever present. A war to expel Iraq from Kuwait would be the United States' first large-scale military conflict since its defeat in Vietnam. Substantial American casualties were a distinct possibility for the first time in almost two decades. It was not an option to be exercised lightly. Fortunately, many thought economic coercion was a feasible alternative.

Although most were aware that sanctions did not have a particularly stellar track record, there were grounds for greater optimism in this case. First, few nations have ever been as isolated as Iraq was in the fall of 1990. It had no friends or allies. A few weak pariahs such as North Korea and Libya might lend some help, but that was about it. The near unanimity of world opinion against Iraq was a solid foundation on which to forge a genuinely broad coalition to impose sanctions that would inflict real pain. Second, Iraq was economically vulnerable. Virtually all of its export earnings came from the sale of oil. Saddled with debt from a nearly decade-long war with Iran, Iraq desperately needed money. Largely because of that war, Iraq was a "crippled nation. From the prosperous country with $35 billion in foreign exchange reserve in 1980, Iraq had been reduced to dire economic straits, with $80 billion in debt and shattered economic infrastructure."[58]

Indeed, Iraq's dire economic straits largely prompted its invasion of Kuwait in the first place. In the months before the attack, the Kuwaitis had rebuffed Iraqi financial demands (e.g., forgiving loans Iraq incurred during its war with Iran) and ignored complaints that they were overproducing oil, thus lowering the price and depressing Iraqi oil revenues. If Iraq could be prevented from selling its (and Kuwait's) oil, this was a potentially devastating blow. This combination of great power agreement generated by the invasion of Kuwait and Iraq's economic vulnerability created an almost unique situation. If economic sanctions could not work under such promising circumstances, it is hard to imagine when they ever would.

It did not take long for a comprehensive sanctions regime to take shape through the United Nations, although a handful of countries were concerned. Japan, highly dependent on imported oil, worried about the consequences of rising prices if Iraqi/Kuwati oil was kept off the global market. Brazil, which sold cars to Iraq and imported a lot of Iraqi oil, was nervous. Turkey was concerned because a third of its oil came from Iraq and a critical pipeline bringing Iraqi oil to market ran through the country. Within a week, however, "a full economic embargo of Iraq had been agreed to . . . Resolution 661 was adopted on 6 August . . . prohibit[ing] all trade with Iraq and Kuwait and any transfer of funds," save medical and humanitarian supplies.[59] Turkey and Saudi Arabia even agreed to cut off the pipelines through which the vast majority of Iraqi oil flowed. The scope of the sanctions and speed with which they were imposed was unprecedented.

Although this was certainly a promising start, there was no guarantee of success. There was no real disagreement that sanctions should at least be given a chance before any resort to military force. A withdrawal induced by sanctions was clearly preferable to one compelled by force.

---

58. Lawrence Freedman and Efraim Karsh, *The Gulf Conflict, 1990–1991: Diplomacy and War in the New World Order* (Princeton, NJ: Princeton University Press, 1993), p. 39.

59. Freedman and Karsh, *The Gulf Conflict, 1990–1991*, pp. 83–84.

continued

But although there was evidence by mid-September that "the economic noose looped around Saddam's neck is clearly having an impact," many doubted this would be enough.[60] The key questions related to mechanisms and timing. That is, how precisely would sanctions bring about an Iraqi withdrawal and how long would it take?

How would the economic pain of sanctions translate into Iraqi action? There were two possibilities. Their impact might be severe enough to incentivize powerful actors and factions within Iraq to oust Saddam and leave Kuwait once he was out of the picture. Alternatively, Saddam himself might be persuaded to change course. That is, sanctions could succeed by changing either Saddam's regime or his mind. For those skeptical of sanctions, neither seemed likely. The Iraqi military, the most likely source of a coup, was well insulated from any hardship. It was also difficult to imagine that Saddam would make a humiliating retreat. The loss of face would be unimaginable. By the end of November there was not the slightest sign of an Iraqi withdrawal:

> Are the economic sanctions beginning to bite in Iraq? From the evidence gathered by the State Department and other agencies, the answer appears to be yes. But are the sanctions biting enough to begin to achieve their goal of changing the behavior of President Saddam Hussein? The answer is apparently no. And in fact, Saddam may be using them to achieve a kind of Battle of Britain mentality, lining up popular support for his defiant stand against the outside world.[61]

In the end, the debate about sanctions came down to a question of time—how long would it take for them to work? Of course, three months is not long, and those who favored sanctions were convinced that their cumulative pain would ultimately outweigh whatever benefits came with the conquest of Kuwait. Senator Sam Nunn (D-GA), chairman of the Senate Armed Services Committee, wanted to see "more analysis done on whether the embargo is going to work and when it's going to work." But even without additional analysis he was convinced "that when you cut off 98 percent of the income of a country, eventually it's going to work if you give it time."[62] In testimony before Nunn's committee at the end of

---

60. Hobart Bowen, "Why Sanctions Might Not Be Enough," *Washington Post* (September 13, 1990), p. A23.
61. Jim Anderson, "Mixed Verdict on Effectiveness of Economic Sanctions," *United Press International* (November 28, 1990).
62. Ibid.

continued

November, two former chairmen of the Joint Chiefs of Staff agreed. According to Admiral William Crowe (ret.), "the issue is not whether an embargo will work but whether we have the patience to let it take effect." What "a sad commentary it would be," he noted dramatically, "if a two-bit tyrant [proved] more patient than the United States, the world's most affluent and powerful nation."[63]

Skeptics wondered how much "patience" would be required. Jeffrey Schott, coauthor of one of the definitive studies of economic sanctions, estimated that it could take as long as one or two years.[64] Few people even ventured a guess, simply expressing a conviction that sanctions would work "eventually." The fear was that leaks would begin to appear in the dike long before sanctions brought Saddam to his knees. Stories of hardships endured by ordinary Iraqis could gradually undermine support for the sanctions on humanitarian grounds. Perhaps more important, "the demand for oil will eventually overpower resentment at the seizure of Kuwait in the international community."[65] No one could know whether the impressive sanctions would last the two years (or however long it would take) or gradually unravel for humanitarian and/or economic self-interest reasons.

Just days after Admiral Crowe urged more time for sanctions, it became clear that the administration was losing its patience when Secretary of Defense Cheney countered Crowe's testimony, arguing that "there is no guarantee that sanctions will force him out of Kuwait . . . Given the nature of the regime, given Saddam Hussein's brutality to his own people, his very tight control of that society, his ability to allocate resources for the military, their ability to produce their own food basically inside, he can ride them out."[66]

Since sanctions were not going to work quickly and there was no guarantee they would work at all, delay risked the worst of all outcomes. It is all well and good to counsel patience, but as the invasion receded into history the outrage it sparked would no doubt wane. If sanctions

---

63. Michael Ross, "Ex-Joint Chiefs Back Gulf Delay," *Los Angeles Times* (November 29, 1990). Accessed at http://articles.latimes.com/1990-11-29/news/mn-7442_1_special-session/.
64. John Maggs, "Sanctions against Iraq Could Work, Study Says," *Journal of Commerce* (November 30, 1990), p. 3A.
65. Gerald Utting, "Iraq Sanctions Will Work?" *Toronto Star* (August 11, 1990), p. D1.
66. Michael Gordon, "Mideast Tensions: Cheney Sees Need to Act Militarily against the Iraqis," *The New York Times* (December 4, 1990). Accessed at http://www.nytimes.com/1990/12/04/world/mideast-tensions-cheney-sees-need-to-act-militarily-against-the-iraqis.html/.

continued

failed to get Iraq out after two years, would the military option remain politically viable? By time the failure of sanctions became clear, the only alternative for getting Iraq out of Kuwait could well be off the table, giving Saddam the fait accompli he hoped to achieve initially. All the while, U.S. forces would have to stay in Saudi Arabia as a deterrent.

The final decision fell to President George H. W. Bush. Fearing that the administration was drifting into war without giving sanctions a real chance, the chairman of the Joint Chiefs of Staff, Colin Powell, met with the president to lay out the logic of sanctions and how they could achieve an Iraqi withdrawal without the costs and uncertainties of war, an option for which there was also no guarantee of success. Bush listened intently but was ultimately unmoved. "Well Colin," he responded, "that's all very, very interesting. It's good to consider all the options. But I just do not think we're going to have time for sanctions to work."[67] War it would be. On January 17, 1991, just a little more than five months after sanctions were imposed, the United States began bombing Iraq. By the end of February, Iraq had been forced of Kuwait.

Present: Economic Sanctions and Iran, 2006–?

In early April 2015, after almost a decade of economic sanctions and eighteen months of arduous negotiations, the United States, Iran, and five other major powers announced a framework for an agreement to be finalized by the end of June that would prevent Iran from developing nuclear weapons while maintaining its right and capacity to develop nuclear power. There was still much work to be done in translating a general framework into a final agreement. Many, particularly in Israel and the United States, remained skeptical and unconvinced that Iran had really abandoned its quest for nuclear weapons. There was still a lot that could go wrong. There were many devils to be found in the details. Several outstanding issues could derail progress toward a final agreement. There was no doubt, however, that the announcement was a potentially critical turning point in the international effort to prevent Iranian nuclearization. If it is ultimately successful, it might also represent a rare success for economic sanctions as an instrument of U.S. foreign policy.

Over the preceding decade, if there was one issue uniting U.S. politicians of all stripes in an era of intense partisan and ideological

---

67. Interview with Colin Powell, *Frontline (PBS): The Gulf War* (January 9, 1996). Accessed at http://www.pbs.org/wgbh/pages/frontline/gulf/oral/powell/1.html/.

continued

polarization, it was that Iran must not be allowed to acquire nuclear weapons. President George W. Bush was blunt, declaring that the United States "will not tolerate the construction of a nuclear weapon" that would place the entire region "under the shadow of a nuclear holocaust." His successor, Barack Obama, was no less adamant, arguing that "we cannot allow Iran to get a nuclear weapon." Former UN Ambassador Bill Richardson's assessment that "stopping Iran's nuclear weapons is a vital American national security interest" would meet with little dissent in Washington.[68] Although outside the political realm some contend that the dangers of a nuclear Iran are wildly exaggerated, most discussion of U.S. policy toward Iran is predicated on the assumption that, as former Secretary of State Clinton declared, Iran with nuclear weapons is simply "unacceptable."[69] Of course, this has not prevented intense debate about, and criticism of, U.S policy. But as was the case with Iraq in 1990–1991, the arguments have mostly about means, not ends—*how*, not *whether*, to prevent Iranian nuclearization. The policy question is also much the same: could economic sanctions and diplomacy dissuade Iran from developing nuclear weapons (if that is the intent) or would a military option be necessary?[70]

Iran has been subjected to economic sanctions since the seizure of hostages from the U.S. embassy in Teheran following the 1979 Islamic revolution. This breach of international law led the United States to impose sanctions that remained in place even after the hostages were released in January 1981. Sanctions motivated primarily by Iran's nuclear activities are more recent, beginning in 2006 when the UN Security Council passed the first in a series of resolutions after an International Atomic Energy Agency report raised concerns about Iran's compliance with the Nuclear Non-Proliferation Treaty (NPT). The main problem was Iran's enrichment of uranium, one of the most critical steps in developing nuclear weapons.

As a signatory of the NPT, Iran is obligated to refrain from acquiring nuclear weapons. Although it can withdraw from the treaty (as North

---

68. Michael Tracey, "Democrats Endorse Crippling Sanction on Iran," *The American Conservative* (September 7, 2012). Accessed at http://www.theamericanconservative.com/democrats-endorse-crippling-sanctions-on-iran/.
69. Quotes from Bush, Obama, and Clinton in Ido Oren, "Why Has the United States Not Bombed Iran?," *Cambridge Review of International Affairs* (December 2011), p. 660.
70. The best case for military option is probably Matthew Kroenig, *Time to Attack: The Looming Iranian Nuclear Threat* (New York: Palgrave–Macmillan, 2014).

continued

Korea did in 2003), Iran has not done so. Iran maintains that it is only interested in nuclear power, which is explicitly permitted by the NPT. Given the overlap between the requirements for nuclear power and weapons, telling the difference can be difficult. Most international observers, however, were skeptical that nuclear power is Iran's only objective, although the definitive "smoking gun" proving otherwise was elusive.[71] Sanctions were intended to pressure Iran into being more forthcoming about its activities and, ultimately, to comply with the NPT. Additional sanctions imposed over the next few years by the United Nations, the United States, and the European Union reflected continuing dissatisfaction with Iran's response.

As is always the case with economic sanctions, debates about their possible success focused on two issues: the amount of pain that could be inflicted and how much Iran was willing to endure. On the first issue, there were reasons to be optimistic. Like any country that gets a large percentage of its income from the sale of one commodity, Iran was potentially vulnerable to sanctions restricting its ability sell or produce it. Although Iran's economy was slightly more diversified than Iraq's in 1990, it was still heavily reliant on oil exports. It also appeared that concern about Iran's nuclear program was sufficient to bring enough countries on board. Getting the United Nations to approve sanctions was a turning point. "The unprecedented degree of international unity against Iran's nuclear program," one analyst noted, "can be seen in the imposition of UN Security Council sanctions, which require approval by Russia and China, nations which have previously been reluctant to sanction Iran."[72] Although it is true that some of the more stringent restrictions were imposed unilaterally by the United States and/or the European Union without Russia and China, there was still good reason to think the overall sanctions regime would enjoy enough international support to hit hard.

Although recognizing these favorable factors, some suspected Iran would be able to mitigate the impact of sanctions and muddle through as work on nuclear weapons progressed. Portraying Iran as "a nation of sophisticated traders," Thomas Ricks predicted that it would "undertake

---

71. A good recent overview of Iran's nuclear program is Jeremy Bernstein, *Nuclear Iran* (Boston: Harvard University Press, 2014).
72. Laicie Heeley and Usha Sahay, *Are Sanctions on Iran Working? Center for Arms Control and Non-Proliferation* (June 3, 2013), p. 6.

continued

a web of evasive measures to struggle on."[73] In this respect, Iran's reliance on oil was a mixed blessing. Although it made Iran vulnerable to sanctions, any reduction in oil production and exports would reduce the supply and raise the price for countries like China and India. Iran might feel the most pain, but others would be hurt as well. In that case, what would China or India want more—a nonnuclear Iran or oil? When the thirst for Iranian oil was combined with black markets and clever ways to get around sanctions, there might well be an opportunity for Iran to reduce their cost.

Even so, there was no doubt that sanctions took quite a toll. *The Economist* reports, for example, that already bad conditions worsened considerably after 2011 when the United States and Western Europe imposed "the most stringent sanctions regimes ever." Once the United States "banned the clearing of dollar payments . . . by Iran's central bank and anyone dealing with it . . . imported industrial components became impossible to get hold of, fuelling unemployment and inflation." Perhaps most important, "Iran's main oil customers in Europe stopped buying almost overnight . . . Oil exports, which in 2011 had been running at about 2.5 m barrels a day, declined by at least half." As a result, "in one week in October 2012 the currency plunged by 40% against the dollar in the black market, creating panic. At its lowest point the rial was down 75%. Unemployment has rocketed. Car production, which used to account for 10% of GDP and employ 1m people, fell by about 70%." But after thirty-four years of sanctions Iranians were used to going without and even with strict sanctions they were "not going hungry and the economy [was] nowhere near collapse."[74]

By 2012 there was clear economic pain without any apparent change in behavior. "If the objective is to change the Iranian leadership's strategic decision to continue developing its nuclear program," Dina Esfandiary noted, "then clearly, they have not worked."[75] Although clandestine programs of sabotage and sophisticated computer viruses may have set the Iranians back some, the goal was to convince the Iranians to abandon

---

73. Thomas Ricks, "Time to Get Serious about Sanctions on Iran," *Foreign Policy* (January 17, 2012). Accessed at http://ricks.foreignpolicy.com/posts/2012/01/17/ time_to_get_serious_about_sanctions_on_iran_especially_through_lebanese_banks/.
74. "Melons for Everyone (Special Report on Iran)," *The Economist* (November 1, 2014), p. 11.
75. Dina Esfandiary, "Actually, the Sanctions on Iran Aren't Working," *The Atlantic* (October 11, 2012). Accessed at http://www.theatlantic.com/international/archive/2012/10/ actually-the-sanctions-on-iran-arent-working/263474/.

continued

their quest for nuclear weapons, not just throw up roadblocks to impede their progress.[76] But more than half a decade after the first UN sanctions, the lack of results appeared to confirm the common wisdom that they seldom work.

This evaluation began to change with election of Hassan Rouhani as president of Iran in 2013, replacing the widely loathed Mahmoud Ahmadinejad. Although the candidates, all approved by Iran's religious leaders, reflected a fairly narrow range of outlooks, Rouhani was seen as the relatively moderate reformist who campaigned on "an explicit mandate to resolve the nuclear issue and improve the economy." His surprisingly large margin of victory was interpreted as a defeat for those determined to move forward with nuclear weapons at any cost: "Iran's hard-liners may be prepared to 'eat grass' if necessary to obtain a nuclear weapon … [but] mounting public dissatisfaction over food shortages and skyrocketing inflation seems to have left doubt about their citizens' willingness to join them."[77] This dissatisfaction was expressed through Rouhani's election.

Once Rouhani took office, negotiations over Iran's nuclear program were revived, leading quickly to an interim agreement in January 2014 in which Iran would cease uranium enrichment.[78] Although temporary, this was still Iran's first concession since UN sanctions were imposed in 2006. For those who thought sanctions could bring about a change in Iranian policy over time, this was a positive sign. Nonetheless, "for all the pundits' valedictories surrounding the apparent success of Iran sanctions," one analyst cautioned, "it is worth noting that they have not in fact yet produced a durable resolution to the nuclear impasse."[79] As of the fall of 2014, the key issue remained whether sanctions could raise the cost of Iran's nuclear program too high for the regime to bear. The costs were high, but were they high enough? This gets to the second part of the equation—how much pain was Iran willing to endure? The underlying

76. Roula Khalaf, James Blitz, Daniel Dombey, Tobias Buck, and Najmeh Bozorgmehr, "The Sabotaging of Iran," *Financial Times* (February 11, 2012). Accessed at http://www.ft.com/intl/cms/s/2/7d8ce4c2-34b5-11e0-9ebc-00144feabdc0.html#axzz3ICjmtVVe/.

77. Suzanne Maloney, "Why 'Iran Style' Sanctions Worked against Tehran (and Why They Might Not Succeed with Moscow)," *Brookings Blog* (March 21, 2014). Accessed at http://www.brookings.edu/blogs/iran-at-saban/posts/2014/03/21-iran-sanctions-russia-crimea-nuclear/.

78. Scott Peterson, "Iran Halts Most Sensitive Nuclear Work, Triggering US, EU Sanctions Relief," *Christian Science Monitor* (January 20, 2014). Accessed at http://www.csmonitor.com/World/Security-Watch/2014/0120/Iran-halts-most-sensitive-nuclear-work-triggering-US-EU-sanctions-relief/.

79. Suzanne Maloney, "Why 'Iran Style' Sanctions Worked against Tehran."

continued

logic of sanctions assumes that targets undertake a cost/benefit calculus. That is, Iranian leaders would pursue nuclear weapons until the costs of sanctions exceeded the expected benefits of going nuclear.

Some worried, however, that this tipping point would never arrive because Iranian leaders did not calculate like this. Israeli Prime Minister Benjamin Netanyahu's skepticism about sanctions rested on a belief that Iranian leaders were not weighing costs and benefits in a rational, strategic fashion. "You don't want a messianic apocalyptic cult controlling atomic bombs," he warned, because "when the wide-eyed believer gets hold of the reins of power and the weapons of mass death, then the world should start worrying, and that's what is happening in Iran."[80] If Iran, or at least its religious leadership, was indeed a cult seeking nuclear weapons to carry out some apocalyptic fantasy that might include the destruction of Israel, sanctions were doomed to fail because the normal cost/benefits calculations on which they rely for success do not apply.

Even if Iran's leaders did weigh costs and benefits, there was no guarantee the tipping point would be reached. This would depend on the perceived benefits of going nuclear, which raises the question of why Iran wanted nuclear weapons in the first place. This is important because the greater the value placed on nuclear weapons, the less likely sanctions were to work. If, for example, Iran viewed nuclear weapons as absolutely essential for its security, the cost of sanctions would have to be very, perhaps impossibly, high to alter its behavior. But the idea that Iran might feel a need for nuclear weapons to protect its security is seldom entertained in the United States. This is largely because Americans find it difficult to imagine that other countries could possibly view the United States as a threat. From Iran's perspective, however, things might look different. Having been singled out as one of three members of the "axis of evil" and seeing what U.S. conventional military power accomplished in Iraq and Afghanistan (which border Iran to the east and west), it would not be unreasonable if Iran's leaders thought nuclear weapons would provide a security guarantee. Just look at the other members of the axis—Saddam, who did not have nuclear weapons, is gone; the Kim dynasty in North Korea, which probably does have a few, plods on. No wonder Iranians often observe that "it's better to be North Korea than Iraq."[81]

---

80. Jeffrey Goldberg, "The Point of No Return," *The Atlantic* (September 2010), p. 58.
81. Vali Nasr, "Why Iran May Be Ready to Deal," *New York Times* (March 17, 2013). Accessed at http://www.nytimes.com/2013/03/18/opinion/why-iran-may-be-ready-to-deal.html?_r=1&/

continued

MAP 4.1: Iran's Location vis-a-vis Other Regional Nuclear Powers

Knowing it could never match the United States' conventional capabilities, Iran could well have believed that only "nuclear weapons would
deter foreign military strikes targeting the Iranian homeland."[82] And even
if the United States was not Iran's major security concern, it lives in a
neighborhood with four of the world's nuclear powers—that is, Israel,
Russia, Pakistan, and India. Would the United States abstain from acquiring nuclear weapons if it faced a similar situation? If Iran sees its nuclear
program as a security requirement—that is, a vital interest—it is difficult
to imagine sanctions being painful enough for it relent.

There are, of course, many other reasons Iran might want nuclear
weapons. Perhaps they are symbols of prestige and status intended to
enhance Iran's image as a regional power, a demonstration of Iran's ability to do what no other Muslim nation in the Middle East has done—enter
the elite nuclear club. For a country that has long considered itself de-
serving of greater respect and influence, this alone could be a powerful

---

82. Clifton Sherrill, "Why Iran Wants the Bomb and What It Means for U.S. Policy," *Nonproliferation
Review* (March 2012), p. 40.

continued

motivation. Aaron Miller and Jason Brodsky think that prestige and security both drove Iranian behavior: "The mullahs see Iran's status as a nuclear weapons state as a hedge against regime change and as consistent with its regional status as a great power."[83]

Domestic political considerations cannot be discounted either. However much Iranians complain about the economic hardship of sanctions, the nuclear program apparently enjoys widespread public support, almost as a matter of national pride.[84] The willingness of the regime to stand up to the world, particularly the United States and Israel, resonates with deep-seated nationalist sentiment in ways Iran's leaders might find useful and difficult to turn away from. It is easy to understand why Iranians would reject the idea that they should be forever denied weapons several of their close neighbors, the United States, and Israel already possess and plan to keep. From this perspective, sanctions are merely "the latest attempt of the West to deny Iran its due respect."[85] What, Iranians might wonder, would be consequences of crying uncle because its arm was being twisted? The United States is not the only country that worries about its image, credibility, and how potential enemies might be emboldened by displays of weakness.

This final point also reveals how intertwined the pieces of the foreign policy puzzle can be. Although it might be analytically useful to explore the dilemmas of interests, threats, and tools separately, in the real world they are linked. Judging whether economic sanctions would be effective inevitably entails assessments of Iranian intentions on at least two levels. The entire sanctions regime assumed that Iran wanted nuclear weapons, which it consistently denied. Although most outside Iran dismiss these denials, not everyone is so sure.[86] But intentions involve more than just *whether* Iran wants nuclear weapons. The more difficult question is *why*,

83. Aaron David Miller and Jason Brodsky, "4 Big Reasons the Iranian Nuclear Deal Didn't Happen," *Foreign Policy* (November 24, 2014). Accessed at http://www.foreignpolicy.com/articles/2014/11/24/4_big_reasons_the_iranian_nuclear_deal_didn_t_happen_zarif_kerry/.
84. See Sarah Beth Elson and Alireza Nader, *What Do Iranians Think? A Survey of Attitudes on the United States, the Nuclear Program and the Economy* (Santa Monica, CA: Rand, 2010), and Max Fisher, "New Poll: Iranians Mostly Blame the U.S. for Sanctions, Still Want a Nuclear Program," *Washington Post* (February 8, 2013). Accessed at http://www.washingtonpost.com/blogs/worldviews/wp/2013/02/08/new-poll-iranians-mostly-blame-the-u-s-for-sanctions-still-want-a-nuclear-program/.
85. Sherrill, "Why Iran Wants the Bomb and What It Means for U.S. Policy," p. 41.
86. See, for example, Seyed Hossein Mousavian, "Ten Reasons Iran Does Not Want the Bomb," *The National Interest* (December 4, 2012). Accessed at http://nationalinterest.org/commentary/ten-reasons-iran-doesnt-want-the-bomb-7802/.

continued

because this will determine whether the pain of sanctions will, or can ever be, great enough to change Iran's behavior. If the framework announced in April 2015 eventually leads to a lasting agreement preventing Iran from acquiring nuclear weapons, the sanctions would have to be judged sufficiently painful to be successful.

....

CHAPTER 5

Putting the Puzzle Together

Competing Visions for U.S. Foreign Policy

We have discussed three major pieces of the foreign policy puzzle: conceptualizing, identifying, and prioritizing interests; assessing threats; and selecting the most effective tools. These are critical issues anyone interested in foreign policy must think about. This is also where we should look to understand what drives policy debates. Whenever there are disagreements about foreign policy, they are likely rooted in differences on one or more of these underlying issues. And there is almost always debate because the issues are so difficult to address, each posing intellectual challenges that are seldom resolved in a manner that produces consensus.

So far, however, we have been engaged primarily in a process of dissection, examining the pieces of the policy puzzle in some detail to understand the smaller puzzles comprising them. But at some point everything must be brought together. The combination is sometimes referred to as a grand strategy, "a purposeful and coherent set of ideas about what a nation seeks to accomplish in the world, and how it should go about doing so." This "requires a clear understanding of the nature of the international environment, a country's highest goals and interests within that environment, the primary threats to those goals and interests, and the ways that finite resources can be used to deal with competing challenges and opportunities."[1]

---

1. Brands, *What Good Is Grand Strategy?*, p. 3.

131

Often considered the gold standard of foreign policy, analysts constantly fret about whether the United States or a given administration has a grand strategy.[2] Such concerns have been especially evident since the end of the Cold War presented the dilemma of strategizing without a unifying threat. "We have slain a large dragon," former Central Intelligence Agency director James Woolsey remarked, "but now we live in a jungle filled with a bewildering variety of poisonous snakes."[3] Can there be *a* grand strategy for a "bewildering variety" of unconnected threats? How does one articulate a coherent strategy for dealing with threats as varied as Kim Jung-Un's North Korea, Vladimir Putin's Russia, a rising China, and the Islamic state?

Grand strategizing is an immensely complicated task even for professionals, never mind amateurs, and any effort to present alternative "grand strategies" is fraught with peril for several reasons. First, few people actually adhere to grand strategies in the sense of a holistic and coherent intellectual framework. At best, views about foreign policy tend to be collections of often loosely connected beliefs, predispositions, or orientations that fail to achieve the high bar of grand strategy. Second, as tidy and distinct as alternative strategies appear on paper, the real world is almost always messier. People combine elements of strategies in ways that do not fall neatly into any typology, and within the broad parameters of strategies there are endless gradations, variations, and exceptions. One recent symposium, for example, with four prominent scholars and policy makers yielded (surprise!) four different strategies.[4] Consequently, any relatively brief survey of alternative strategies will be illustrative, not exhaustive or comprehensive.

Keeping these caveats in mind, the focus here is on three contending perspectives/strategies. The first, often referred to as "restraint" or "offshore balancing," challenges widely held views most sharply in recommending a significantly diminished global role for the United States. The other two represent variations of the prevailing consensus in favor of an internationalist foreign policy in which the United States

2. See, for example, Daniel Drezner, "Does Obama Have a Grand Strategy?: Why We Need Doctrines in Uncertain Times," *Foreign Affairs* (July–August 2011), pp. 57–68.

3. Ibid., p. 146.

4. Richard Fontaine and Kristin Lord, eds., *America's Path: Grand Strategy for the Next Generation* (Washington, D.C.: Center for a New American Security, 2012).

remains actively and deeply involved politically, economically, and militarily. Although these strategies predated the end of the Cold War, they have gradually been recast or restated to reflect differing reactions to the Soviet Union's demise and, after that, the attacks of 9/11 and concerns about terrorism and WMD.

We will see that just as debates on specific issues are almost always rooted in disagreements about interests, threats, and/or tools, so too with grand strategy. A strategy of restraint differs from variants of internationalism that dominate the foreign policy establishment primarily in its narrow view of U.S. vital interests and less alarming assessment of threats. The two versions of internationalism, however, are similar in their definition of U.S. interests, part ways somewhat in their assessment of threats, and diverge most sharply on the question of what policy instruments are likely to be most effective in pursuing U.S. interests and objectives over the long haul.

Restraint: Interests[5]

A strategy of restraint or offshore balancing offers a fairly radical alternative to contemporary American foreign policy, especially in terms of military commitments and the use of force. It rests on the proposition that the United States, by virtue of its fortunate geography, is an unusually secure country. With vast oceans to the east and west and two smaller, friendly countries to the north and south, it is far from any potential adversary. Thanks to its geographic position and powerful nuclear deterrent, distant events are unlikely to snowball or set in motion a chain of events that will endanger the United States. The United States enjoys a large strategic cushion.

This does not mean the United States is invulnerable. Geography no longer affords the same level of safety it did a century ago. In a world of missiles, bombers, and unconventional terrorist attacks, no country enjoys absolute safety. Nonetheless, "geography still matters in national security. . . . the oceans constitute a formidable defense against

---

5. The most recent, and perhaps definitive, statement of this perspective is Barry Posen, *Restraint*. See also Christopher Layne, "America's Middle East Grand Strategy: The Moment for Off-Shore Balancing Has Arrived," *Review of International Studies* (January 2009), pp. 5–25; and Eugene Gholz, Darryl G. Press, and Harvey M. Sapolsky, "Come Home, America: A Strategy of Restraint in the Face of Temptation," *International Security* (Spring 1997), pp. 5–48.

conventional invasion if the United States retains the naval and air power to fight on, above and under them." Whatever threats grab the headlines at any given moment, they should not be allowed to obscure the reality that "the U.S. strategic situation is remarkably good relative to others. It is rich, distant from other great powers, and defended by a powerful nuclear deterrent."[6] Indeed, "by any reasonable measure the United States is the safest country in the history of the world."[7]

Given this reality, the United States' enduring strategic priority— its most vital interest—is what it has always been: ensuring that no distant hostile power controls sufficient resources to overcome the United States' inherent advantages. In practice this means that no hostile state should be allowed to dominate Europe and Asia. Only a power in control of the vast economic and human resources of Eurasia would pose a genuine threat to the security of the United States. As long the resources of Eurasia are divided among friends and foes (or controlled by the former), the United States can afford to adopt an aloof and detached posture.

This has not always been the case. The prospect of German domination in the 1940s and Soviet expansion in the early Cold War necessitated U.S. military involvement in both Europe and Asia because more proximate states were unable to contain these hostile powers on their own. The mere existence of a hostile state, however, is not in and of itself a critical problem. The United States must simply "ensure that key areas of the world aren't dominated by hostile powers."[8] If local powers friendly to the United States can prevent this, great. If they cannot, then it is time for the United States to engage, to step in from its offshore position to balance against the threat.

"Key areas" are those possessing the combination of human, economic, and technological resources necessary to influence the global distribution of power—that is, Europe and East Asia. The one exception to this formulation is the Middle East, whose unique importance rests on one particularly critical commodity. Consequently, a strategy

6. Posen, *Restraint*, pp. 19 and 23.

7. Fettweis, *The Pathologies of Power*, p. 25. See also Micah Zenko and Michael A. Cohen, "Clear and Present Safety: The United States Is More Secure Than Washington Thinks," *Foreign Affairs* (March/April 2012), pp. 79–83.

8. G. John Ikenberry and Stephen Walt, "Off-Shore Balancing or International Institutions (A Debate)," *Brown Journal of World Affairs* (Fall/Winter 2007), p. 14.

of restraint usually includes the need to prevent a hostile power from dominating the Persian Gulf. Adding this to the overall strategic equation, Layne provides the best summary of what interests are vital for the United States:

> Offshore balancing is based on the assumption that the most vital US interests are preventing the emergence of a dominant power in Europe and East Asia—a "Eurasian hegemon"—and forestalling the emergence of a regional ("oil") hegemon in the Middle East. Only a Eurasian hegemon could pose an existential threat to the US. A regional hegemon in the Middle East could imperil the flow of oil upon which the US economy, and the economies of the advanced industrial states depend.[9]

In terms of preventing a "Eurasian hegemon," the good news is that there is no plausible candidate. Russia is a mere shadow of the former Soviet Union beset by a host of internal problems. No doubt it has caused trouble for some its neighbors (most of which used to be part of the Soviet Union), but it is not in any position to aspire to continental hegemony.

The more serious candidate is China, whose potential is certainly immense. As Posen notes, "the Soviet Union never had an economy more than about half as productive as the United States. China could ultimately prove a much more formidable economic and strategic competitor."[10] The operative word here, however, is "ultimately." Although more than two decades of substantial economic growth has brought China to the point where it is about to surpass the United States (in aggregate, not per capita, terms), it is still a country with many domestic challenges to tackle to remain on its current trajectory. It is certainly a power to be watched closely, but there is no immediate danger of it becoming a Eurasian hegemon.

The other good news is that regional powers have plenty of resources to counter Russia and/or China. We are no longer in the immediate post–World War II period with war-ravaged countries unable to stand on their own. Japan, South Korea, Taiwan, and India possess the human and economic resources to counter China in its current state, and India already has its own nuclear arsenal (as does one of

9. Layne, "America's Middle East Grand Strategy," p. 8.
10. Posen, *Restraint*, p. 18.

China's other neighbors, Russia). In Europe the situation is even better, with some of the world's most affluent countries whose resources are more than sufficient to counter their neighbor to the east: "whatever residual threat Russia poses to Europe could easily be addressed by Europeans themselves."[11] Germany, France, and Great Britain on their own have larger economies than Russia. Taken together, their economy is four times larger than that of Russia. It strains credulity to think they are unable to counter whatever threat Russia presents.

The Middle East is more complex but by no means unmanageable. Although the "US does have an interest in preventing the emergence of a Persian Gulf oil hegemon, the risk of such a development is low, because the three largest states in the Gulf—Saudi Arabia, Iraq, and Iran—lack the military capabilities to conquer each other." Furthermore, "because of its overwhelming military capabilities compared to the big three Gulf powers, the US easily could deter any of them from launching a war of conquest" without a constant military presence in the region.[12]

The bad news, particularly in Europe and Asia, is that regional powers have grown accustomed to relying on the United States. Why should they increase defense spending to counter local threats when the United States will do it? They have become used to free-riding (or at least cheap-riding) on the United States. Too often, much of U.S. defense spending "amounts to a subsidy to other prosperous nations that could defend themselves if they spent a little more on defense."[13] These friends and allies must be incentivized to act on their own. Whatever threat emerges in Europe and Asia to U.S. interests will be an even greater threat to these more proximate powers. Although it should be gradual, perhaps taking as long as a decade, "American withdrawal would force U.S. allies to accept political responsibility for managing their own affairs."[14]

Restraint: Nuclear Proliferation

Advocates of strategic restraint tend to be less worried about nuclear proliferation than most. Indeed, in some cases they consider nuclear

11. Ibid., p. 34.
12. Layne, "America's Middle East Grand Strategy," p. 13.
13. Ibid., p. 27.
14. Gholz et al., "Come Home, America," p. 15.

proliferation desirable, even necessary. If the United States withdraws its forces from Europe and East Asia, regional powers would need to confront China and Russia, both nuclear powers. No longer protected by the U.S. nuclear "umbrella," they might well want their own nuclear arsenals. Germany, Japan, and South Korea could be tempted to go nuclear. There is little to worry about, however, because all of these countries have the economic and technological wherewithal to maintain safe nuclear forces and the survivable retaliatory capabilities needed for deterrence.

From the U.S. perspective, South Korea with nuclear weapons may not be worrisome, but what about Iran or other "rogue states"? Although this might be unwelcome, there is always the option of deterrence. Even with dramatic post–Cold War reductions, the United States retains a sizable nuclear arsenal. Presumably, it does not intend to use these weapons aggressively. They function as a deterrent. And since there is no need to deter friends or states that would never consider using their weapons against the United States, one must assume that the purpose is to deter enemies and adversaries who might actually contemplate attacking the United States.

Those who favor a strategy of restraint and withdrawal generally believe that nuclear deterrence works and is robust. Whatever outrageous comments leaders of rogue states may make in public, they understand the consequences of nuclear retaliation that could eviscerate the countries they lead. Past rogue leaders, such as China's Mao Tse-Tung, grasped this harsh reality and acted with appropriate restraint. Today many forget how dangerous a nuclear China once appeared. As Paul Pillar reminds us, "China's development of a nuclear weapon (it tested its first one in 1964) seemed all the more alarming at the time because of Mao's openly professed belief that his country could lose half its population in a nuclear war and still come out victorious over capitalism." Despite such alarming rhetoric, "deterrence with China has endured for half a century, even during the chaos and fanaticism of Mao's Cultural Revolution."[15] There is no reason to think the mullahs in Teheran will be any different should they join the nuclear club.

Complaining that the United States appears "fixated on preventing nuclear proliferation," Posen thinks it should just accept the reality

---

15. Paul Pillar, "We Can Live with a Nuclear Iran," *The Washington Monthly* (March/April 2012), p. 15.

that "nuclear weapons are a modern fact of life: states that possess them will want to keep them, and some states that do not presently have them will probably get them," partly because "they permit small states to defend their sovereignty against large ones."[16] The United States might not like this, and it may be worth taking some steps (e.g., sanctions) to complicate the efforts of countries like Iran to acquire nuclear weapons. But because deterrence remains an option if they do, preventing the acquisition of nuclear weapons does not rise to the level of a *vital* national interest. Just because something is desirable does not mean it is vital.

Nuclear weapons in the hands of terrorist groups, however, would be something to worry about. "Ensuring that only states with return addresses possess nuclear devices," Posen concedes, "is a significant U.S. strategic interest."[17] Nonetheless, he tends to discount the possibility that a state would hand off nuclear weapons to terrorist organizations. States do not make large investments in developing such awesome weapons only to hand them over to groups they cannot control. And even if the terrorist groups themselves are difficult, perhaps impossible, to deter once they have such weapons, the United States can still make credible deterrent threats against states that might be inclined to provide them: "States with nuclear materials need to understand that if they give them away and they are used, retaliation will be directed at the source."[18]

Restraint: Terrorism

For the advocates of restraint/offshore balancing, states continue to be the most important players in international relations. States alone possess the resources to genuinely threaten U.S. security. This is not to say that nonstate actors (in this context a euphemism for terrorist groups) pose no danger. The attacks of September 11 proved that they do. Although "the threats of greatest importance arise from other nation-states. . . . private organizations can do great harm through terrorism, their capacity pales against the potential of nation-states."[19] But however dramatic the occasional terrorist attack might be and no matter

---

16. Posen, *Restraint*, p. 73.
17. Ibid., p. 72.
18. Ibid., p. 81.
19. Ibid., p. 1.

how much fear it might instill, al-Qaeda and similar groups are not the Soviet Union or Nazi Germany. They do not have the capacity to endanger American security and safety in the same way. They do not pose an existential threat. The threat of terrorism has been exaggerated out of all proportion because the attacks themselves can be so horrific in human terms. Their psychological impact exceeds their actual significance—that is, they terrorize people, which is the essence of terrorism. But as Walt argues,

> People have to recognize that terrorism is not an enemy; it's just a tactic. As long as terrorist groups do not get weapons of mass destruction, they cannot threaten the U.S. way of life or fundamentally alter the trajectory of our society, unless we voluntarily let them. It's still a major problem we have to act on, but we should keep the threat in perspective. You could even imagine something like 9/11 happening once a decade; that would be awful, but it wouldn't end the United States as we know it.[20]

Furthermore, terrorist attacks and hostility toward the United States did not just emerge from nowhere. Although it is common to argue that terrorists hate the United States for what it is and stands for, advocates of restraint think it is also a response to U.S. policies, a reaction to U.S. domination, hegemony, and intervention, especially in the Middle East:

> Terrorism is [an] asymmetric strategy—one employed by non-state actors like Al-Qaeda and similar jihadist groups—to resist US dominance. The use of asymmetric strategies to oppose American power—especially in the Middle East where US policy has an imperial dimension—illustrates the dictum that empires inevitably provoke resistance.[21]

In the Middle East "there is good reason to believe a high and martial profile helps generate antipathy to the United States, which may create a more supportive environment for the more violent and determined enemies."[22] Indeed, "were the United States not so intimately involved in the affairs of the Middle East, it's hardly likely that the

20. Ikenberry and Walt, "Off-Shore Balancing or International Institutions (A Debate)," p. 18.
21. Layne, "America's Middle East Grand Strategy," pp. 7 and 9.
22. Posen, *Restraint*, p. 133.

detestation would have manifested itself as violently as it did on 9/11."[23] Thus, a policy of "restraint should reduce the incentive of terrorists to attack the United States." But even this "will not stop all attacks against U.S. targets."[24]

The direct use of military force may occasionally be the most appropriate response. Advocates of restraint are not pacifists. There was a good case to be made for going after al-Qaeda in Afghanistan immediately after the September 11 attacks. The mistake was expanding the mission to include the transformation of Afghanistan, a complicated nation-building project that went well beyond the requirements of counterterrorism. Terrorist groups are usually best handled by good intelligence and cooperative efforts to undermine their activities with only occasional and highly focused uses of force, and an effort to eliminate the "root causes" of terrorism (assuming we even know what they are) by fundamentally changing the political, social, and economic fabric of other countries or entire regions is likely to be an expensive and ultimately frustrating fool's errand.

Restraint: Values and Interests

As should be evident, a strategy of restraint entails a "limited set of political objectives abroad and more limited means to achieve them."[25] It rests on an admirably clear, but some fear excessively narrow, view of U.S. vital interests: preventing a hostile power from dominating and controlling the resources of either Eurasia or the Persian Gulf. The "limited set of political objectives abroad" includes those directly related to U.S. national/physical security. Absent from this strategy are any explicitly moral or humanitarian objectives beyond this. A strategy of restraint has no missionary element. Indeed, any suggestion that the United States spread democracy and its political values to other states, particularly by military force, is dismissed as dangerous and hubristic idealism. Restraint or offshore balancing "eschews the ideological crusading on behalf of democracy that is endemic to Wilsonianism, [and] defines US interests in terms of what is vital rather than simply

23. Christopher Layne and Bradley A. Thayer, *American Empire: A Debate* (New York: Routledge, 2007), p. 70.

24. Gholz et al., "Come Home, America," p. 30.

25. Rosen, *Restraint*, p. 166.

desirable."[26] However desirable spreading democracy might be, it is not vital. Walt warns that democracy promotion is a recipe for endless meddling:

> Liberals think that it is an important U.S. interest to mold the international order and to mold the internal politics of other countries. That's part of the agenda—you've got to shove other countries in the direction of democracy. The problem is that once you start taking on that agenda, it starts to become very hard to restrain yourself, particularly when you're as powerful as the United States currently is.[27]

Democracy promotion is also a recipe for disappointment when applied to societies where the foundations for successful democratization are lacking. The decidedly mixed (to be charitable) results of a decade-long effort to bring democracy to Iraq and Afghanistan are the most prominent cases in point. More important, U.S. security simply does not depend on distant nations sharing our values and political institutions. If they do, great. If they do not, it is regrettable but not necessarily dangerous. In the final analysis, "America's freedom from physical attack or coercion does not depend on peace in Africa, democracy in Latin American, or human rights in Cambodia."[28]

A strategy of restraint or offshore balancing would represent a truly radical departure for U.S. foreign policy. Perhaps for this reason alone it is often recognized as an interesting option but seldom embraced. It represents an intellectual challenge to prevailing wisdom but does not seem like a realistic option. Critics often dismiss it as isolationism, a term that conjures up the 1930s with intimations of appeasement. Despite frequent concessions that the United States should not be the "world's policeman," few are willing to contemplate such a fundamental departure from the post–World War II norm. There appears to be little enthusiasm for the United States abandoning its leading role in the world. The need for some form of U.S. leadership is usually taken as a given, but this means different things to different people.

26. Layne, "America's Middle East Grand Strategy," p. 8.
27. Ikenberry and Walt, "Off-Shore Balancing or International Institutions (A Debate)," p. 22.
28. Gholz et al., "Come Home, America," p. 40.

Primacy: Interests

The first vision of American leadership emerged as the Cold War came to an end. Rather than retreat in the face of a diminished threat, a strategy of primacy called for the United States to expand its global ambitions. The United States needed to exploit its unique position not only to combat a series of deceptively smaller threats that were in some senses even more dangerous than those faced during the Cold War, but also to look beyond the horizon to prevent the emergence of future threats by maintaining an intimidating level of military superiority and spreading democracy. This strategy embodied an expansive view of U.S. interests/objectives, an alarming assessment of threats, and a belief that military power was essential for countering these threats and preventing the emergence of new ones.

A strategy of primacy was first articulated within the government in a series of Department of Defense policy planning guidelines leaked to the *New York Times* in 1992.[29] The guidelines represented an early effort to think through the implications of the Soviet Union's collapse. The primary recommendation, the "first objective" it identified moving forward, was "to prevent any hostile power from dominating a region whose resources would, under consolidated control, be sufficient to generate global power. These regions include Western Europe, East Asia, the territory of the former Soviet Union, and Southwest Asia [the Middle East]." The guideline's authors, however, saw no immediate cause for alarm because "it is improbable that global conventional challenge to U.S. and Western security interests will remerge from the Eurasian heartland for many years to come."[30] There was nothing terribly new or controversial in this. Preventing the emergence of a Eurasian hegemon has long been seen as a vital U.S. interest. The judgment that there was no credible candidate for Eurasian hegemony in the

---

29. Charles Krauthammer, "The Unipolar Moment," *Foreign Affairs: American and the World* 70 (1990–1991), pp. 23–33. On the Defense planning papers, see James Mann, *The Rise of the Vulcans: The History of Bush's War Cabinet* (New York: Viking, 2004), pp. 208–215; Patrick Tyler, "Excerpts from the Pentagon's Plan: 'Prevent the Reemergence of a New Rival," *New York Times* (March 8, 1992), p. A18; Barton Gellman, "Keeping the U.S. First: The Pentagon Would Preclude a Rival Superpower," *The Washington Post* (March 11, 1992); David Armstrong, "Dick Cheney's Song of America: Drafting a Plan for Global Dominance," *Harper's* (January 2003).

30. Patrick Tyler, "Excerpts from the Pentagon's Plan," p. A18.

foreseeable future was also widely shared. Even those who favored a strategy of restraint and withdrawal agreed with both of these points. More controversial than the objective was the recommendation for achieving it: "we must maintain the mechanisms for deterring potential competitors from even aspiring to a larger regional or global role." That is, despite the Soviet Union's collapse, American military dominance needed to be sustained or even increased to dissuade states from challenging the United States globally or regionally. Whereas a strategy of restraint viewed the Soviet Union's demise as a reason for U.S. withdrawal from Eurasia, a strategy of primacy entailed maintaining a U.S. presence and overwhelming military power to convince potential adversaries that it was futile to even contemplate competing with the United States. Having won the last race, the United States should keep its foot on the gas so that no one dare start or join a new one.

Although the uproar accompanying the leaked documents led the Bush administration to distance itself, others were eager to carry the banner of primacy, including many who would later become known as "neoconservatives."[31] In their view, military power was not something to keep in reserve for the sole purpose of intimidating potential competitors. Although it was certainly useful for this, military power was also a big stick to be used, not just carried, in pursuit of important interests and objectives. In a globalized age of WMD, ballistic missiles, and terrorism, vital U.S. interests are not limited to the absence of a Eurasian hegemon. This was only the bare minimum. And given the resources at its disposal, there was no reason for the United States to settle for the bare minimum.

Advocates of primacy warn of the dangers of instability and violence in critical regions even without the prospect of domination by

---

31. On neoconservatism generally, see Justin Vaisse, *Why Neoconservatism Still Matters* (Washington, D.C.: Brookings Institution, 2010); Justin Vaisse, *Neoconservatism: The Biography of a Movement* (Cambridge, MA: Harvard University Press, 2010); John Ehrman, *The Rise of Neoconservatism: Intellectuals and Foreign Affairs, 1945–1994* (New Haven, CT: Yale University Press, 1996); Gary Dorrien, *The Neoconservative Mind: Politics, Culture, and the War of Ideology* (Philadelphia: Temple University Press, 1993); Gary Dorrien, *Imperial Designs: Neoconservatism and the New Pax Americana* (New York: Routledge, 2004); Danny Cooper, *Neoconservatism and American Foreign Policy: A Critical Analysis* (New York: Routledge, 2011); and, of course, Stefan Harper and Jonathan Clarke, *American Alone: The Neo-Conservatives and the Global Order* (Cambridge, MA: Cambridge University Press, 2005).

hostile states. The mere fact that there is no adversarial hegemon in Eurasia or the Persian Gulf would be cold comfort if these regions were racked by instability, violence, conflict, war, and proliferating WMD. Maybe this would not pose a genuinely existential threat to the United States in the strictest sense. Geography and a massive nuclear arsenal might insulate it from the worst effects of instability on the other side of the world. Its survival as an independent state might not be endangered. But would this be the kind of world in which Americans want to live? Could they prosper in such an uncongenial environment? Primacists think not. The United States thus has a vital interest in preserving a certain measure of international order, stability, and peace. These are valuable ends in and of themselves.

Whereas advocates of restraint assume that a U.S. withdrawal would incentivize local powers to deal with regional problems and threats, primacists have no such confidence. They fear that other states will continue to shirk their responsibilities, allowing problems to fester and threats to grow. In their view, U.S. hegemony and power are absolutely critical for the preservation of international order and stability. According to Krauthammer, for example, "international stability is never a given . . . it is never the norm." When stability is achieved, "it is the product of self-conscious action by the great powers, and most particularly of the greatest power, which is now and for the foreseeable future the United States." "The world," he warns, "does not sort itself out on its own."[32] Kristol and Kagan echo the sentiment, arguing that "the appropriate goal of American foreign policy . . . is to preserve [U.S.] hegemony as far into the future as possible" because "American hegemony is the only reliable defense against a breakdown of peace and international order."[33]

The U.S. interest in international stability should also be forward looking. Rather than keeping its powder dry while "passively waiting for the next threat to arrive," a strategy of primacy entails an ambitious agenda for addressing the underlying conditions that give rise to these threats.[34] With respect to the Middle East, "we could continue to fight Arab/Islamic radicalism by catching a terrorist leader here, rolling up

32. Krauthammer, "The Unipolar Moment," p. 29.
33. William Kristol and Robert Kagan, "Toward a Neo-Reaganite Foreign Policy," *Foreign Affairs* (July/August 1996), p. 23.
34. Ibid., p. 27.

a cell there. Or we could go to the heart of the problem and take the risky but imperative course of trying to reorder the Arab world."[35] What is the "heart of the problem"? On a political level, it is undemocratic, corrupt, and repressive regimes that stifle dissent, breeding frustration and anger that finds an outlet in radicalism and terrorism.

As long as the underlying conditions go unaddressed, there will always be new leaders and cells to chase, trapping the United States in endless game of whack-a-mole, tackling symptoms while the disease goes untreated. In the long run, the United States will face far fewer dangers to its security and international stability if it can expand the scope of democracy.[36] Thus, "the task facing us is to preserve and extend the democratic era as far into the future as possible. The present moment is one of relative safety, and therefore one that offers special opportunities. It would be a timeless human tragedy if, out of boredom, laziness, carelessness, or unfounded gloom, we failed to seize them."[37]

Thus, in addition to preventing the rise of a hostile Eurasian or Middle Eastern hegemon, the United States has a vital interest in international order and stability as well as creating a foundation for future peace and stability by spreading democracy. Although these are U.S. interests, primacists are quick to point out that they are also universal goods and values. U.S. interests and ideals coincide with those of others around the world. A policy of primacy reflects an enlightened self-interest that benefits all, not crass selfishness in which the United States' gains come at the expense of others. This is why the world is expected to welcome, not resist, American power. U.S. dominance is, and will be, seen as a "benign" or "benevolent" hegemony.

Primacy: Threats

It was difficult for anyone to deny that the Soviet Union's collapse altered the United States' threat environment. Largely for this reason,

---

35. Charles Krauthammer, "In Defense of Democratic Realism," *The National Interest* (Fall 2004), p. 23.

36. See Joshua Muravchik, *Exporting Democracy: Fulfilling America's Destiny* (Washington, D.C.: American Enterprise Institute, 1991), and Gregory A. Fossedal, *The Democratic Imperative: Exporting the American Revolution* (New York: Basic Books, 1989).

37. Robert Kagan, "Democracies and Double Standards," *Commentary* (August 1997), p. 25.

Kagan conceded in 1997 that the United States was "relatively safe." Kristol and Kagan similarly noted "the lack of a visible threat to U.S. vital interests or world peace." They brushed aside "the ubiquitous post–Cold War question—where is the threat?" as "misconceived." The best answer they could muster was that "the main threat the United States faces now and in the future is its own weakness," a clever response revealing the absence of threats.[38] Although Krauthammer recognized the United States "has no great power enemies," he saw emerging dangers. "The post–Cold War era," he thought, would become the "era of weapons of mass destruction" in which "the rise of small aggressive states armed with weapons of mass destruction . . . makes the coming decades a time of heightened, not diminished, threat of war."[39] Although they were quick to remind everyone that threats remained, primacists saw the immediate post–Cold War world more in terms of the opportunities than the threats. That fortune state of affairs did not last long.

The attacks of September 11 changed all this, bringing together concerns about rogue states, Islamic fundamentalism, the proliferation of WMD, and terrorism. When the radicalism and hostility toward the United States motivating al-Qaeda were combined with the possible acquisition of WMD, primacists saw a new existential threat to the United States. Sure, it was not the same type of threat a Eurasian hegemon would pose. No terrorist group was going to invade or occupy the United States. But this is not the only kind of existential danger. Again it was Krauthammer who crystalized the new threat assessment best. In his view, "radical Islam . . . [is] as fanatical and unappeasable in its anti-Americanism, anti-Westernism and anti-modernism as anything we have known." After September 11 it became clear that "radical Islam's obvious intent is to decapitate the American polity, cripple its economy and create general devastation." If terrorist groups driven by this ideology got their hands on a few biological or nuclear weapons, the consequences could be catastrophic:

> Imagine what a dozen innocuous vans in a dozen American cities dispersing aerosolized anthrax could do. Imagine what just a handful of the world's loose nukes, detonated simultaneously in New

---

38. Kristol and Kagan, "Toward a Neo-Reaganite Foreign Policy," p. 23.
39. Krauthammer, "The Unipolar Moment Revisited," p. 8, and "The Unipolar Moment," pp. 31 and 23.

York, Washington, Chicago and just a few other cities, would do to the United States. America would still exist on the map. But what kind of country—and what kind of polity—would be left? If that is not an existential threat, nothing is.[40]

Consequently, every link in the chain that might contribute to this outcome was a vital concern to the United States. The groups themselves must be targeted and eliminated. The social, economic, and political conditions that give rise to them and ensure a steady stream of recruits must be addressed. The proliferation of WMD to states that might sympathize with terrorist groups must be prevented. More important, primacists rejected as outdated the idea that only other states can pose an existential danger to a geographically blessed United States.

Primacy: Tools

Primacists are most commonly criticized for their willingness, even eagerness, to use military force. Although some of the more extreme charges of militarism may be slightly overdrawn, primacists clearly display a greater confidence in the efficacy of military force than other grand strategies. When Kristol and Kagan explicitly rejected John Quincy Adams' admonition that the United States should "not go abroad in search of monsters to destroy," they asked "why not?" "The alternative," they argued, "was to leave monsters on the loose, ravaging and pillaging to their heart's content, as Americans stand by." Because the United States "has the capacity to contain or destroy many of the world's monsters . . . a policy of sitting atop a hill and leading by example becomes in practice a policy of cowardice and dishonor."[41] Although they do not explicitly endorse the use of military force to destroy all these monsters, it is a reasonable surmise that they are unlikely to be destroyed or deterred by softer means. Whether in Iraq, Syria, Libya, or Iran, support for military action is most likely to be found among primacists.

---

40. Krauthammer, "In Defense of Democratic Realism," p. 18. A similar assessment can be found in Norman Podhoretz's lengthy and appropriately titled essay, "World War IV: How It Started, What It Means, and Why We Have to Win," *Commentary* (September 2004), pp. 17–51.

41. Kristol and Kagan, "Toward a Neo-Reaganite Foreign Policy," p. 31.

None of this is to say that primacists think military force is the solution to every problem or that they are always in agreement on particular uses for force. Although they were in near universal agreement favoring of the 2003 Iraq war, this has not always been the case. Many supported NATO's air campaign against Serbia in 1999, whereas a few dissented. Even those who accept the same basic strategy can nonetheless make different judgments about the wisdom of specific actions. It is also important to point out that primacists are not alone in their willingness to support the use of force. Even in the case of the Iraq war, which was closely associated with primacists/neoconservatives, support extended well beyond their ranks, as evidenced by the fairly bipartisan endorsement it received in Congress. Nonetheless, "what distinguishes neoconservatives [i.e., primacists] from traditional liberals is that we're more ready to resort to the use of hard power."[42]

It is not only a greater confidence in the efficacy of military force that distinguishes primacists/neoconservatives but also a willingness to use it unilaterally without international sanction or approval. The ability to act alone when needed is a benefit of the United States' tremendous advantage in military power that should not be compromised. Primacists realize assistance from other nations and the sanction of international organizations can be useful but warn against viewing either as a prerequisite. This is partly a reflection of the low esteem in which they hold most international organizations, particularly the United Nations. At a deeper level, it reflects a suspicion of anything limiting the United States' freedom of action. Primacists insist that the United States "must be guided by its own independent judgment, both about its own interests and the global interest . . . America should neither defer nor contract out its decision-making, particularly when concessions involve permanent structural constrictions." Otherwise it will become a "[tied] down Gulliver with a myriad of strings that will diminish his overweening power."[43]

Liberal Internationalism: Interests

Primacists tend toward the conservative end of the political spectrum, although familiar political labels do not always align neatly in foreign

---

42. An Interview with Joshua Muravchik, *Democratiya* (Winter 2007), p. 275.
43. Krauthammer, "The Unipolar Moment Revisited," pp. 5–17 at 12 and 14.

policy strategies. Some of the most prominent advocates of restraint, such as Christopher Layne, consider themselves conservatives. On the other side of the spectrum we typically find some variation on what is commonly referred to as liberal internationalism. But despite being on opposite ends, primacy and liberal internationalism actually share much in common, particularly in their view of U.S. interests and objectives.[44] Indeed, for those who favor a substantially diminished role for the United States, the differences between the two versions of internationalism pale in comparison to the similarities. Rieff, for example, is almost dismissive, describing their disagreements as "more in the nature of an internationalist family quarrel than a fundamental difference."[45] And Betts describes liberal internationalism as "soft primacy."[46]

Like primacists, liberal internationalists did not see the Cold War's end as a reason for the United States to shed its Cold War commitments. Yes, much of American foreign policy since the end of World War II was focused on containing the Soviet Union, so its demise should have led to some rethinking of priorities. Nonetheless, it is a mistake to see the United States' security commitments and the larger web of political, economic, and military institutions it helped build during the Cold War solely in terms of containing the Soviet Union. Even if this was a significant impetus for their creation, there were larger purposes and interests transcending the Soviet threat that remained equally important after it had passed.

G. John Ikenberry focuses on the larger picture, explaining how during the Cold War "the United States took the lead in fashioning a world of multilateral rules, institutions, open markets, democratic

---

44. A good starting point for understanding liberal internationalism as a foreign policy strategy is the work of G. John Ikenberry, most notably his *Liberal Leviathan: The Origins, Crisis and Future of the American World Order* (Princeton, NJ: Princeton University Press, 2012); *After Victory: Institutions, Strategic Restraint, and the Rebuilding of Order after Major Wars* (Princeton, NJ: Princeton University Press, 2000), especially Chapters 6 and 7; and "Liberal Internationalism 3.0: American and the Dilemmas of Liberal World Order," *Perspectives on Politics* (March 2009), pp. 71–87.

45. Quoted in Robert Kagan, "Neocon Nation: *Neoconservatism c. 1776*," *World Affairs* (Spring 2008), p. 26.

46. Richard K. Betts, "American Grand Strategy: Grand v. Grandiose," in Richard Fontaine and Kristin M. Lord, eds., *America's Path: Grand Strategy for the Next Administration* (Washington, D.C.: Center for a New American Century, 2012), p. 35.

community, and regional partnerships—and put itself at the center of it all." This order was "remarkably successful." In geopolitical terms, it kept the Soviet Union in check while averting a potentially apocalyptic war between the superpowers. Beyond this, "it provided a stable foundation for decades of Western and global growth and advancement. The United States and its partners negotiated agreements and built mechanisms that reopened the world economy, ushering in a golden age of economic growth."[47] It was an order based on "a set of institutions and relationships that have allowed the world to live together in more peaceful and mutually beneficial ways than any other type of order or era of world history."[48] For liberal internationalists, the end of the Cold War was no reason to throw this all away.

In terms of seeing a critical interest in maintaining a stable, politically democratic, and economically open and prosperous international order, primacists and liberal internationalists are largely in agreement. And although talk of U.S. "hegemony" or "primacy" is often avoided, liberal internationalists also a see a continued need for what they prefer to characterize as American "leadership." They may not go as far as portraying the United States as "the only reliable defense against a breakdown of peace and international order," but they do think that "the United States must continue to provide global leadership" because "without such leadership, solutions to global collective action problems . . . are unlikely to arise." Primacists warn that the world does not "sort itself out," and liberal internationals caution that "if the leader does not lead, things do not get done."[49]

Like primacists, liberal internationalists worry about the consequences of American withdrawal on the scale envisioned in a strategy of restraint. Even without a Eurasian hegemon on the horizon, U.S. alliances and security guarantees are useful, perhaps necessary, for dampening security competition and preventing arms races among regional powers. In proposing U.S. retrenchment, Posen predicted that current allies would increase their military capabilities substantially in

47. Ikenberry, *Liberal Leviathan*, pp. 29 and 2.

48. "Interview/G. John Ikenberry: Liberal International Order Should Be Strengthened to Integrate a Rising China," *The Asahi Shimbun* (September 13, 2013). Accessed at http://ajw.asahi.com/article/views/opinion/AJ201309130001/.

49. Robert Art, "Selective Engagement in an Era of Austerity," in Richard Fontaine and Kristin M. Lord, eds., *America's Path: Grand Strategy for the Next Administration* (Washington, D.C.: Center for a New American Century, 2012), p. 19.

response. A few would probably even move to acquire nuclear weapons. He thought this would be a good thing. Liberal internationalists are not so sure.

Looking back over the Cold War, for example, Nye shares Ikenberry's view that the combination of Cold War military, political, and economic institutions was beneficial beyond pure geopolitics. Citing the remarkable post–World War II economic development of countries like Japan and South Korea, he thinks that "among the important and often neglected reasons for East Asia's success are American alliances in the region and the continued presence of substantial U.S. forces." He expressed anxiety about what might happen if U.S. forces left the region, posing a rhetorical question revealing his fears: "Will there be a political order and security framework that will sustain this impressive economic growth, or will the stable expectations of entrepreneurs and investors be subverted first by costly arms races and then by armed conflicts?"[50]

At a minimum, this kind of retrenchment would be a huge leap into the dark, a big gamble probably not worth taking. Since the United States played such a central role in the creation of this international order, there is no telling what could happen if it was removed from the equation. Are the savings that would accrue to the United States by removing its forces worth the potential costs in terms of arms races and instability? Could the international order from which the United States and others benefit so much survive or would it unravel like a garment once the wrong thread is pulled? Liberal internationalists would rather not find out.

Thus, we can see that primacists and liberal internationalists share a similar conception of U.S. interests and objectives. Since primacists are often considered "conservative," this might seem odd to many. But as Posen and Ross explain, "though primacy is focused on the maintenance of overwhelming U.S. power and influence, it remains strongly committed to liberal principles."[51] Common liberal principles coupled with a belief that active and intensive U.S. leadership is needed to preserve international order and stability leads many to lump the two

---

50. Joseph Nye, "The Case for Deep Engagement," *Foreign Affairs* (July–August 1995), p. 91.

51. Barry R. Posen and Andrew L. Ross, "Competing Visions for U.S. Grand Strategy," *International Security* (Winter 1996/97), p. 34.

strategies together. Posen, for example, presents just one alternative to his strategy of restraint, an all-encompassing "liberal hegemony." This is why Rieff viewed them as branches of the same "interventionist family." But what is the family quarreling about?

It is possible to see some difference in the assessment of threat. Although both primacists and liberal internationalists emphasize the same dangers—rogue states, terrorism inspired by radical Islamic fundamentalism, and the proliferation of WMD in volatile regions—primacists tend to see them individually and collectively as more severe than liberal internationalists. Although liberal internationalists would generally prefer, for example, that Iran not obtain nuclear weapons, most think it would be susceptible to the normal dynamics of deterrence if it did. And although Islamic terrorism is recognized as a problem, there is little talk of it being an existential threat. These differences in threat assessment are, however, not dramatic and certainly not sufficient on their own to draw any sharp distinction. It is more a matter of degree, nuance, and emphasis. The two part company most significantly on means—that is, how the United States should defend its interests and pursue its objectives in light of these threats.

Liberal Internationalism: Tools

For Rieff, the debate between primacists and liberal internationalists is "not about principles at all but rather about which form of Wilsonianism—hard or soft, bound to rules of America's own making or contemptuous even of these rules—best furthers America's interests in the world." Although they both endorse U.S. leadership, liberal internationalists are "more respectful of and reliant on international institutions and international law, more decently modest in its expression, and far, far more skeptical of the role of the use of force."[52] Perhaps because he rejects their shared Wilsonianism, Rieff recognizes but remains unimpressed by these differences.[53] On some level this is probably correct, but for liberal internationalists the distinction is not so

---

52. "Debating Liberal Internationalism," *The American Prospect* (May 15, 2008). Accessed at http://prospect.org/article/debating-liberal-internationalism/.

53. Rieff is not alone in this regard. See also Tony Smith, *America's Mission: The United States and the Worldwide Struggle for Democracy* (Princeton, NY: Princeton University Press, 2012, expanded edition), pp. 346–383.

trivial. What is at stake is whether the United States behaves in a manner that undermines or sustains its leadership over the long haul. Here the use of leadership becomes significant in conveying something different than hegemony. Betts makes the point in noting that "it is a mistake . . . to equate leadership with imposing U.S. control or ensuring good outcomes on all important issues. Attempts to control generate resentment and resistance."[54] Leadership, unlike hegemony, presumes the existence of followers. The challenge of U.S. foreign policy lies in convincing others that they should follow, persuading them that their interests and American interests coincide, and providing reasons to regard U.S. leadership as legitimate. Others must view the United States as using its power to achieve mutually beneficial and desirable ends, not abusing it to run roughshod over the interests and wishes of others.

To this end, liberal internationalists think the United States should generally refrain from unilateral uses of force, work within and through the international institutions it helped create, and abide by the rules and norms it expects others to obey. If Gulliver insists that no ropes restrict his movement, why should anyone else tolerate restraints? This might be okay as long as Gulliver can get his way by his own might, but what happens when he needs others? Derek Chollet gets to the heart of the matter in identifying the "core concept of liberal internationalism" as "legitimacy." For "America to project its power and maintain leadership . . . [it] needs to offer others a reason to have some allegiance to it beyond its sheer power."[55] For liberal internationalists the sort of aggressive, some might say arrogant, hegemony associated with primacists is unlikely to attract many followers or much allegiance no matter how benevolent Americans think it is. No one wants to be part of an American "empire," even if the emperor has noble intentions.[56] Primacists, however, scoff at such concerns as "goo-goo one-worldism" that will lead to the "domestication of American power," inhibiting the United States' ability to maintain order and counter threats others are unwilling or unable to tackle.[57]

54. Betts, "American Grand Strategy: Grand v. Grandiose," p. 35.

55. "Debating Liberal Internationalism."

56. See Max Boot, "The Case for American Empire," *The Weekly Standard* (October 15, 2001), pp. 27–30.

57. Krauthammer, "The Unipolar Moment Revisited," p. 13.

If this all sounds familiar, it should. The liberal internationalist emphasis on acting within the framework of institutions and abiding by rules and norms to maintain the legitimacy of its leadership required in the long term reflects a belief in the importance of soft power. Indeed, legitimacy can be seen as another word for, or at least a major component of, soft power. Concerns about the connection between U.S. conduct and legitimacy were heightened, of course, by the 2003 Iraq war. Not surprisingly, it was Nye who drove home the point:

> Meeting the challenge posed by trans-national military organizations that could acquire weapons of mass destruction requires the cooperation of other countries and cooperation . . . similarly, efforts to promote democracy in Iraq and elsewhere will require the help of others. Reconstruction in Iraq and peacekeeping in failed states are far more likely to succeed and to be less costly if shared with others . . . the fact that the United States squandered its soft power in the way that it went to war meant that the aftermath turned out to be much more costly than it need have been.[58]

This is not to say that unilateral U.S. action will never be needed. The argument is simply that the United States' interests in the long run are served by exercising leadership in a manner that elicits approval and support, particularly with respect to allies in critical regions. Ikenberry looks to successes of the past for lessons: "The secret of the United States' long brilliant run as the world's leading state was its ability and willingness to exercise power within alliance and multinational frameworks, which made its power and agenda more acceptable to allies and other key states around the world."[59] Thus, primacists and liberal internationalists disagree not about U.S. interests and the need for U.S. leadership, but about the forms of power that are most likely to sustain the United States' leadership and protect its interests.

Conclusion

We began this book by pointing out that any public policy presents both intellectual and political challenges. Invoking Corwin's observation about the "invitation to struggle for the privilege of directing

---

58. Nye, "Soft Power and American Foreign Policy," p. 259.
59. G. John Ikenberry, "America's Imperial Ambition," *Foreign Affairs* (September/October 2002), p. 56.

American foreign policy," we noted that there are really two invitations and struggles, one political and the other intellectual. This book accepted the second invitation. The focus has been on the central challenges in thinking about what U.S. foreign policy ought to be. Emphasizing the identification of interests, assessment of threats, and selection of tools, the goal was to explain and illustrate why these elements of foreign policy are so central and difficult and why consensus is so elusive. This should help the reader think about the dilemmas of foreign policy with a greater level of self-awareness and analyze policy debates more systematically.

In conclusion, however, it is useful to return to the invitation declined and recognize the magnitude of the political challenges remaining once the intellectual challenges have been tackled. Betts, after laying out his ideas for U.S. grand strategy, warns that "the U.S. Constitution is, in effect, anti-strategic." By anti-strategic he means that as difficult as it is for strategists to bring the pieces of the foreign policy puzzle together into a coherent, unified strategy, it is even more difficult for the U.S. government to adopt and implement a national grand strategy. Channeling Corwin, he explains that because "power is diffused widely, checks and balances frustrate or sidetrack initiatives, legislative and executive authority changes hands frequently, [and] government is often divided . . . objectives are pursued consistently only when a durable consensus about them exists."[60]

Bett's warning suggests that the intensity of the political struggle surrounding U.S. foreign policy varies with the intensity of the intellectual struggle. Consensus on policy and strategy could ameliorate, although probably not completely eliminate, the fractious, anti-strategic tendencies of American governance. The prospects for the emergence of a foreign policy consensus, however, do not appear great. The larger point is that the struggle surrounding U.S. foreign policy has two equally important and interrelated sources—the anti-strategic structure and dynamics of the U.S. political system and the inherent difficulty of achieving consensus on policy and strategy.

---

60. Betts, "American Grand Strategy: Grand v. Grandiose," p. 32.

INDEX

....

Note: page numbers followed by *f* and *t* refer to figures and tables respectively; those followed by n refer to notes, with note number.

and Soviet intentions, difficulty of
determining, 65–66, 74–75,
76–77, 79, 81–85
and U.S. credibility, necessity of
defending, 41–42
U.S. soft power and, 113, 115
U.S. support for authoritarian
regimes during, 6, 44, 45
Vietnam War and, 52
and West Berlin, U.S. defense of,
40, 41–42, 55
Commission on America's National
Interests
on prevention of genocide as
national interest, 35*t*, 48–50
ranking of U.S. interests by, 32–36,
35*t*, 42
Committee on the Present
Danger, 84
communism, Morgenthau on varieties
of, 56–57
communist aggression, as threat to
Middle East stability, 6
Congress
powers of, as point of
contention, xvi
resistance to soft power
spending, 114
containment policy
Chinese rise and, 88–89
Cold War Soviet threat to Europe
and, 65–66
continuity conundrum, 77
Corwin, Edwin, xvi, 154–155
cost of tools of influence
in Iraq War, as issue, 21–23,
22n48, 24
as issue in evaluating specific
tools, 20
counterinsurgency wars, debate on
necessity of fighting, 97
credibility of U.S.
defense of, and interest inflation,
38–39, 41–42, 43

and difficulty of disengaging from
unsuccessful conflict, 102103
Korean War and, 38–39, 42
Syrian civil war and, 62, 63
U.S. ability to further interests
and, 36
Vietnam War and, 42, 54–55,
57–58
Crimea, sanctions against Russia for
annexation of, 109–110
Crowe, William, 121
Cuba, sanctions on, 105–106
culture, as source of soft power, 94

Dahl, Robert, 93
Debs, Alexandre, 10–11
democracy
defining of national interest in, 28
in Middle East, U.S. efforts toward,
8, 45
primacy strategy on spreading of,
142, 145
restraint strategy on spreading of,
140–141
Department of Defense, 142
détente with Soviet Union, Soviet
intentions as issue in, 81–85
deterrence
of Iraqi use of WMDs, as issue,
16–20, 20–21, 23, 24
Iraqi WMDs as, in Gulf War, 118
military power as, 106
of terrorist use of WMDs, as issue,
17, 138
U.S. nuclear weapons as, 137–138
diplomacy
inferring other nations' intentions
from, 67–69
interest inflation in, 36–37
domino theory, Cold War and, 39–40,
41–42, 53–55
Drezner, Daniel, 109–110
Drum, Kevin, 116
Dulles, John Foster, 38–39, 41

Index 163

vital
  efforts to identify, 32–36, 35*t*
  interest inflation and, 33, 34,
    35–36, 36–43, 50–51
  in liberal internationalism
    strategy, 148–152
  as overused term, 25–26
  in primacy strategy, 142–148
  in restraint strategy, 133–136,
    140–141
  in war on terrorism, prioritization
    of, as issue, 12–13
International Energy Agency, and
  sanctions on Iran, 122
international institutions. *See also*
  stability, international
  liberal internationalism on,
    149–150, 151, 152–154
  primacy strategy on, 148, 153
Iran
  and "axis of evil," 127
  Islamic revolution in (1979),
    6, 122
  and neighbors (map), 128*f*
  nuclear weapons program
    domestic support for, 129
    framework agreement on
      (2015), 122, 130
    and intentions, impossibility of
      knowing, 71, 124, 127–130
    interim agreement on
      (2014), 126
    liberal internationalism strategy
      on, 152
    motives for, as issue, 127–130
    restraint strategy on, 137
    and rise of more moderate
      leadership, 126
    and sanctions, 106–107,
      122–130
    skepticism about Iranian
      claims, 122, 129
    U.S. commitment to stop, 122
  threats against Israel, 69

  as threat to Middle East stability,
    6, 18
  as threat to U.S., 2
  U.S. embassy hostages (1979), 122
Iran-Iraq War
  as evidence of Iraqi aggression, 9,
    18–19
  and Iraqi intentions, difficulty of
    determining, 75, 77
  U.S. support of Iraq in, 2, 18
Iraq. *See also* Gulf War (1990–91);
    Hussein, Saddam; Iran-
    Iraq War
  and "axis of evil," 127
  democratization efforts in,
    restraint strategy on, 141
  and intentions, impossibility of
    knowing, 71, 75, 77
  Kuwait invasion by, 2 (*See also*
    Gulf War)
    as evidence of Iraqi aggression,
      9, 19
    expulsion by allied forces
      (Gulf War), 2–4, 69
    motives for, 19, 119
    sanctions following, 105,
      118–122
    U.S. forces in Saudi Arabia and,
      106, 118, 122
  map of, 3*f*
  sanctions against
    after Gulf War, 4, 106, 107
    for invasion of Kuwait, 105,
      118–122
  and WMDs, possession of
    as deterrent in lead-up to Gulf
      War, 118
    general agreement on, before
      Iraq War, 13, 14, 15
    past use of, 13, 19, 63
    as rationale for Iraq War, 7,
      8–12, 10–11n29, 13
    and risk of terrorist WMD
      attacks, 11, 17, 19–20, 72

Saddam's defiance of resolutions
by, 8, 10, 14
and sanctions on Iran, 122, 124
and sanctions on Iraq, 4, 106,
107, 119
United States. *See also* credibility of
U.S.; grand strategy of U.S.;
interests of U.S.; military
power, U.S.; threats to U.S.;
other specific topics
geographical isolation of, and vital
interests, 133–134, 144
and military capacity *vs.* intent, 70
as world policeman, 141
United States Commission on
National Security, 33n15

Vietnam War
arguments of opponents to, 55–58
and difficulty of disengaging from
unsuccessful conflict, 102,
103, 104
domino theory and, 53–55
and limiting of war to vital
interests, 100
outcome of as unsatisfactory, 97
postwar debate on parameters for
use of force, 97
U.S. casualties in, 52
and U.S. credibility, necessity of
defending, 42, 54–55, 57–58
and U.S. interests, prioritizing of,
52–58
U.S. reluctance to use force
following, 118
"Vital Interests: What Are They and
Who Says So?" (Brodie), 27

Walt, Stephen, 25–26, 31, 36, 139, 141
war on terrorism
impact of Iraq war on, as issue, 23
prioritization of U.S. interests in, as
issue, 12–13
weapons of mass destruction.
See WMDs

Weinberger, Caspar, 98
Weinberger Doctrine, 98–101, 104
Wen Jiabao, 87
West Berlin, U.S. defense of, 40,
41–42, 55
WMDs (weapons of mass
destruction)
Iraqi possession of
as deterrent in lead-up to Gulf
War, 118
general agreement on, before
Iraq War, 13, 14, 15
past use of, 13, 19, 63
as rationale for Iraq War, 7,
8–12, 10–11n29, 13
and risk of terrorist WMD
attacks, 11, 17, 19–20, 72
Saddam's calculated effort to
feign, 14–15
U.S. failure to find, impact
of, 112
willingness to use, as issue,
15–17, 19
preventing attack on other nations
by, as U.S. national interest,
35*t*, 48
preventing attack on U.S. by, as
vital national interest, 34,
35*t*, 42
primacy strategy on threat from,
146–147
Wolfers, Arnold, 27
Woolsey, James, 132
World War II
Allied bombing of civilians
in, 107
European withdrawal from Middle
East following, 6
and Marshall Plan, 29–30, 31
mistaken assessment of German
intentions in, 64–65, 68

Young, Milton, 54

Zambernardi, Lorenzo, 57